Instant Pot
Cookbook for Two

Easy and Delicious Everyday Instant Pot Recipes for Two

Jessy Jones

Contents

Introduction

Hello, and welcome to my book of Instant Pot recipes for two! I have all the recipes you need to make delicious and beautiful meals. Whether you're cooking for two, or just for yourself, you've come to the right place. There are a lot of cookbooks available that have recipes to feed a family, but what about when you want to make enough for two people? You've picked up the perfect cookbook for you to cook those smaller meals…and of course still have plenty of leftovers!

It's no different cooking for two than it is for four or more. The only thing you need to change is the quantities of the ingredients. I completely understand that a lot of times you wonder if it's worth it for you to get out those ingredients, prepare, and then cook…just for the two of you. Many times, I've wanted to cook an incredible meal for my partner and me. Then I think of all the work involved. And I decide that quickly making an omelet and toast is much easier and faster.

Well, you can stop thinking that way! This is the great thing about the Instant Pot. It does all the work for you. You need to find the perfect recipe, prepare the ingredients and toss them in the pot. Then sit back and relax while the Instant Pot does its magic. Before you know it, the two of you will be sitting down to a fantastic meal!

What is an Instant Pot?

The Instant Pot is an amazing invention. It makes your life so much easier when it comes to creating great meals. It's ideal for singles, couples, and families. To simplify it, the Instant Pot is an electric pressure cooker that has many different functions and ways to cook foods. You can use it as a slow cooker and a rice cooker. It makes excellent soups and stews. You can use it to steam foods and keep them warm. Some Instant Pot models even come with a function for making yogurt!

Cooking for two is just as satisfying as cooking for more. No matter what you're in the mood for, you'll find the perfect dish in my cookbook!

Instant Pot Benefits

The only kitchen appliance you need

It's expensive to have a variety of different appliances that take up a lot of room in your kitchen... and then there's all the pots and pans. With all the functions the Instant Pot can perform, it's an economic investment that will make more room in your kitchen cupboards when you get rid of the rice cooker and steamer that are just taking up kitchen space.

Easy to use

Using the Instant Pot is as easy as pressing a few buttons. No more complicated recipes that take you forever to read through and then just as long to make. Now the Instant Pot does all the work for you. And my recipes are so easy to follow, without a lot of steps for you to work your way through. The Instant Pot is perfect for couples who aren't professional chefs but who still want to enjoy a great tasting meal at home.

Gets dinner on the table… quickly

The Instant Pot slashes cooking time, so dinner is ready in no time. Using pressure and high temperatures, food cooks quickly and efficiently. You can throw everything together and have a meal prepared in the blink of an eye. Once you use the Instant Pot, you won't be able to live without it! You'll be able to cook roasts and ribs in less than an hour!

Multipurpose

With so many different Instant pot functions you can make different and exciting dishes every night of the week. Creamy soups, delicious stews, juicy roasts, and steamed vegetables. No matter what you're craving, you'll find just the right recipe in my book.

Healthy food

The Instant Pot lets you safely cook healthy meals. By pressure cooking at high temperatures, food cooks in its juices, keeping both flavors and nutrients right in the pot. When you're focusing on eating right, cooking for two has never been so easy The Instant Pot is completely safe to use. When food is prepared, the Instant Pot automatically releases pressure to lower the temperature. Or you can control the pressure by using the release valve.

How to Use Your Instant Pot

Browning meats and chicken

Use the Sauté function to brown and sear meats and chicken before you put them in the Instant Pot. This gives the meat more flavor by sealing in flavor and moisture.

Instant Pot Tip: When using the Sauté function, leave the lid off the Instant Pot.

Adding ingredients to the Instant Pot

Once you have all the ingredients for one of my recipes prepped and ready to go, load up the Instant Pot. Put the harder vegetables on the bottom, followed by meats. Softer vegetables that cook faster go on the top along with liquids. Never fill the pot more than two thirds full.

Reduce wine for rich flavor

You can make great tasting and rich sauces with the Instant Pot. Use the Sauté function to reduce wine before adding the rest of the ingredients to the pot. The alcohol from the wine will evaporate, leaving the wine flavor to infuse the dish with an incredible richness.

Adding liquids

When you're using the Instant Pot as a pressure cooker, you'll need to make sure that you add juice to the pot. As a rule, use at least 1 cup of liquid, such as water, vegetable or beef stock, or canned tomatoes.

Choose the function and get ready to cook

Once you have all the ingredients in the Instant Pot, it's all set to cook. Just twist the lid onto the pot. Choose the cooking function you're going to be using, such as the Soup, Stew, or Rice function. If you're not sure what function you should be using, it's simple. Just use the Manual function, set the time, and let the Instant Pot do its thing.

Set the timer

Follow the instructions in my recipes and set the Instant Pot for the correct time. Just use the plus (+) and minus (-) buttons to adjust. Once the Instant Pot has enough pressure, the timer will start to count down.

Instant Pot Tip: The steam valve should be sealed for all functions except for the Slow Cook function. For the Slow Cook function, the steam valve should be set to vent.

Releasing the pressure

When the timer goes off, you'll know your meal is ready. If you do nothing, the pressure will release on its own after a few minutes. If you want to get your meal on the table sooner, you can release the pressure yourself. Just switch the steam valve from sealed to vent. To prevent injury, use a towel when releasing the pressure.

How to Use the Buttons on Your Instant Pot

There are several cooking mode buttons on the Instant Pot. Understanding them is essential for easy cooking with the Instant Pot.

Manual – Manual is the most used cooking mode and allows you to set your own cooking time.

+ and - – Use these to increase or decrease the cooking time.

Adjust – Use this to adjust the settings to their in-built default mode.

Pressure – Switch between LOW and HIGH pressure.

Keep Warm/Cancel – Use this to either cancel cooking or use your Instant Pot as a warmer to keep your meal warm until ready to serve.

Slow Cook – You can use your Instant Pot as a slow cooker.

Steam – Use to steam veggies. The default is setting is10 minutes.

Yogurt – Use this to make yogurt. You can also pasteurize milk on the less setting, or even make porridges on the more setting.

Rice – Use this to cook rice. This setting automatically cooks on LOW pressure, but you can change that if you like.

Meat/Stew – Default cooking time is 35 minutes. Use this setting for cooking meat and making stews.

Bean/Chili – The default setting is 30 minutes. Use this setting for cooking bean dishes and chilies.

Soup/Broth – The default setting is 30 minutes.

Porridge – If you love porridges you will be pleased to know that you can now make them with a convenient click of a button.

Sauté - Default cooking time is 30 minutes. When using this function, the lid must be left open at all times

Why is the Instant Pot Perfect for Two?

Perfect size

With your Instant Pot, you can make enough for just the two of you to eat for one meal…with a few leftovers for you to take for lunch or another meal.

Harmony in the kitchen

No more arguing about whose turn it is to make dinner. The Instant Pot is so easy to use, you'll both want to impress the other with the delicious meal recipes in my book.

Easy clean-up

Clean-up in the kitchen is super easy with the Instant Pot. You'll only have one pot to clean! You can wash it with warm soapy water. Or even easier – toss it into the dishwasher. Less time in the kitchen is more time doing something else you both want to do.

Great for small kitchens

The Instant Pot is ideal for small kitchens. When you're not using it, you can store it away in a cupboard. Or you can leave it on the counter for your next meal. Remember, when you have an Instant Pot with all those functions, you can get rid of all those other appliances that are just taking up valuable space in your kitchen.

About the Recipes

My recipes are ideal for making a tasty meal for two…with some leftovers for you to enjoy for lunch the next day. Or you can freeze leftovers, so you have a scrumptious dish to quickly reheat when you're in a rush.

The timing of each recipe

Each of my recipes lets you know exactly how long it takes to prep the ingredients and put them into the pot. And then how long it takes for the dish to cook.

Instant Pot Tip: Remember that the timer starts counting down when the correct pressure and temperature in the Instant Pot are reached.

Functions and settings

I've included a variety of recipes in my cookbook…that cover all the functions of your Instant Pot. Each recipe indicates what setting you should use to get the best results.

Quick release or natural release

In many of my recipes, I recommend that you use the Quick Release method of releasing pressure in the Instant Pot. This will get dinner on the table faster than if you use the Natural Release method. When you have time, feel free to use the Natural Release for any recipe.

Cooking fish or vegetables

Use the Quick Release when cooking fish or soft vegetables in the Instant Pot. These foods are easy to overcook, so you want to get them out of the Instant Pot as soon as the timer goes off.

Recipe seasonings

In most of my recipes, for salt and pepper seasoning, I've simply listed the ingredient and left it up to you to decide how much you want to use. Adjust according to your taste. For other seasonings and herbs, such as chili powder and parsley flakes, I've listed exact amounts so that you can duplicate the flavors in my recipes.

Fresh garlic

A quick note on using fresh garlic. Recipes list the amount of garlic I use in a dish. As with other seasonings, feel free to adjust according to how much, or how little, you like a garlicky flavor in your meals.

Breakfast

Bacon and Paprika Scrambled Eggs

(Prep + Cook Time: 15 minutes / Servings: 2)

Ingredients:

1 tsp. basil, chopped

4 eggs

2 oz. bacon, chopped

½ tsp. paprika

½ tsp. salt

Pinch of black pepper

Directions:

1. Whisk together the eggs, spices, cilantro, and basil, in a bowl. Select SAUTÉ.
2. Place the bacon in the Instant Pot and sauté for 3 minutes. Add the egg mixture and cook for 5 more minutes.
3. Scramble the eggs with a wooden spoon and cook for 3 more minutes.

Nutritional Info per Serving: Calories 290, Protein 16, Carbs 4.5, Fat 23.4

Sausage and Cheddar Frittata

(Prep + Cook Time: 20 minutes / Servings: 2)

Ingredients:

¼ cup ground breakfast sausage

1 tbsp. sour cream

¼ cup grated cheddar cheese

2 eggs

1 cup water

Salt and pepper, to taste

Directions:

1. Pour the water into the Instant Pot and lower the rack.
2. Spray a soufflé dish with cooking spray. Whisk together the eggs, sour cream, and some salt and pepper. Stir in the sausage and cheddar cheese.
3. Pour the mixture into the soufflé dish, and cover with aluminum foil. Place on the rack, seal the lid and select MANUAL. Cook for 17 minutes on low pressure.
4. Do a quick pressure release, and serve immediately.

Nutritional Info per Serving: Calories 282, Protein 16, Carbs 1, Fat 12

Creamy Oatmeal with Peaches

(Prep + Cook Time: 15 minutes / Servings: 2)

Ingredients:

1 peach, chopped
2 cups water
1 cup rolled oats

½ tsp. vanilla
1 tbsp. flax meal
½ tbsp. maple syrup

Directions:

1. Place the peach, oats, vanilla, flax meal and maple syrup in your Instant Pot.
2. Stir to combine well. Pour the water and stir again.
3. Seal the lid, select MANUAL, and cook on HIGH for 3 minutes.
4. Allow pressure to release naturally for 10 minutes.
5. Serve and enjoy!

Nutritional Info per Serving: Calories 215, Protein 6, Carbs 37, Fat 3

Pomegranate Porridge

(Prep + Cook Time: 5 minutes / Servings: 2)

Ingredients:

1 cup oats
1 cup pomegranate juice
1 cup water

1 tbsp. pomegranate molasses
Sea salt to taste

Directions:

1. Place the water, oats, salt, and juice in your Instant Pot.
2. Stir to combine and seal the lid.
3. Select MANUAL, and cook for 3 minutes on HIGH.
4. Once ready, do a quick pressure release.
5. Carefully open the lid and stir in the pomegranate molasses.
6. Serve immediately.

Nutritional Info per Serving: Calories 387, Protein 14, Carbs 67, Fat 6

Bacon and Cheddar Egg Muffins

(Prep + Cook Time: 15 minutes / Servings: 2)

Ingredients:

1 cup water
2 bacon slices, cooked and crumbled, divided
⅛ tsp. lemon pepper seasoning
2 eggs

½ scallion, chopped and divided
2 tbsp. shredded cheddar cheese, divided
Salt to taste

Directions:

1. In a bowl, whisk together the eggs, lemon pepper and salt.
2. Divide the cheese onion and bacon, between 2 silicon muffin cups.
3. Then, pour the egg mixture over.
4. Pour the water into your Instant Pot and arrange the muffin cups on the rack.
5. Seal the lid, select MANUAL, and cook on HIGH for 10 minutes.
6. Once ready, do a quick pressure release.
7. Serve and enjoy!

Nutritional Info per Serving: Calories 70, Protein 4.6, Carbs 1.5, Fat 2.4

Bacon and Cheese Hash Brown Breakfast

(Prep + Cook Time: 10 minutes / Servings: 2)

Ingredients:

2 eggs
Salt and black pepper, to taste
½ cup frozen hash browns

2 bacon slices, chopped
⅛ cup milk
¼ cup grated cheddar cheese

Directions:

1. Set the Instant Pot on SAUTÉ mode, add and cook the bacon until crispy, about 2 minutes.
2. Add the hash browns, and cook for 2 more minutes.
3. Whisk the eggs, milk, salt, pepper, and cheese, in a bowl.
4. Pour this mixture over the bacon and hash browns, and seal the lid.
5. Select MANUAL, and cook on HIGH for 5 minutes.
6. Once ready, do a quick pressure release and serve immediately.

Nutritional Info per Serving: Calories 164, Protein 12, Carbs 7, Fat 11

Three Meat Quiche

(Prep + Cook Time: 35 minutes / Servings: 2)

Ingredients:

1 cup water

3 eggs

2 bacon slices, cooked and crumbled

¼ cup milk

¼ cup diced ham

½ cup cooked ground sausage

½ pinch of black pepper

½ cup grated cheddar cheese

1 bunch of green onions, chopped

1 scallion, chopped

Directions:

1. Pour the water in your Instant Pot. Whisk the eggs along with the salt, pepper, and milk, in a bowl.

2. In a 1-quart baking dish, add the bacon, sausage, ham, and mix to combine.

3. Pour the eggs over, and stir to combine again. Sprinkle with green onions and cheese. Cover with foil and place in the Instant Pot. Select MANUAL, and cook on HIGH for 30 minutes.

4. Once ready, do a quick pressure release and serve hot.

Nutritional Info per Serving: Calories 419, Protein 29, Carbs 4.1, Fat 32

Italian Sausage and Peppers

(Prep + Cook Time: 30 minutes / Servings: 2)

Ingredients:

½ tbsp. dried basil

7 oz. tomato sauce

14 oz. canned diced tomatoes

2 green bell peppers, cut into strips

4 Italian sausages

½ cup water

½ tbsp. Italian seasoning

1 tsp. minced garlic

Directions:

1. Pour half a cup of water into your Instant Pot. In a baking dish, place all of the ingredients.

2. Stir to combine. Place the dish in the Instant Pot, and seal the lid.

3. Set on MANUAL and cook on HIGH pressure for 25 minutes.

4. Once ready, do a quick pressure release and serve immediately.

Nutritional Info per Serving: Calories 389, Protein 23, Carbs 8, Fat 29

Simple Steel Cut Oats

(Prep + Cook Time: 10 minutes / Servings: 2)

Ingredients:

1 ½ cups water, divided
½ cup steel cut oats

½ cup milk, warm
1 tsp. sugar

Directions:

1. Pour half a cup of water in your Instant Pot.
2. In a heatproof bowl, combine the oats and 1 cup of water.
3. Place the bowl on the trivet, inside the Instant Pot.
4. Seal the lid, select MANUAL, and cook on HIGH for 6 minutes.
5. Once ready, release the pressure quickly.
6. Carefully open the lid, and stir in the milk and the sugar. Serve warm.

Nutritional Info per Serving: Calories 155, Protein 4, Carbs 28, Fat 2

Banana Bread Oatmeal

(Prep + Cook Time: 25 minutes / Servings: 2)

Ingredients:

½ cup walnuts, chopped
2 cups water
1 cup oatmeal

½ tsp. vanilla
1 banana, mashed
⅛ cup honey

Directions:

1. Place the walnuts, oatmeal, vanilla, bananas, and honey into the Instant Pot.
2. Stir to combine well. Pout the water and stir again.
3. Seal the lid, select PORRIDGE and cook for 10 minutes on HIGH.
4. Once ready, allow pressure to release naturally for 10 minutes.

Nutritional Info per Serving: Calories 370, Protein 10, Carbs 50, Fat 12

Almond and Rolled Oats

(Prep + Cook Time: 10 minutes / Servings: 2)

Ingredients:

1 ½ cups almond milk

¼ cup chopped almonds

½ cup rolled oats

⅛ cup sugar

½ tbsp. coconut oil

1 cups chopped pears

½ Pinch of cinnamon

½ Pinch of salt

Directions:

1. Set your Instant Pot to SAUTÉ mode. Add the coconut oil and melt it.

2. Stir in all of the remaining ingredients. Seal the lid, select MANUAL, and cook on HIGH for 6 minutes.

3. Allow pressure to release naturally for 10 minutes.

Nutritional Info per Serving: Calories 288, Protein 5, Carbs 39, Fat 4.5

Soups

Easy Chicken Soup with Carrots and Potatoes

(Prep + Cook Time: 50 minutes / Servings: 2)

Ingredients:

¼ onion, diced

1 frozen chicken breasts

8 oz. chicken stock

8 oz. water

1 carrot, peeled and chopped

2 potatoes, cubed

Directions:

1. Place the onions, chicken breasts, chicken stock, water, carrot and potatoes into your Instant Pot.

2. Seal the lid, select MANUAL, and cook on HIGH for 35 minutes.

3. Once ready, wait 10 minutes before releasing the pressure quickly.

4. Carefully open the lid and shred the chicken with 2 forks inside the pot.

5. Serve hot and enjoy.

Nutritional Info per Serving: Calories 72, Protein 9, Carbs 7, Fat 8

Instant Pot Vegan Soup

(Prep + Cook Time: 25 minutes / Servings: 2)

Ingredients:

3 oz. broccoli, chopped

1 cup vegetable broth

½ garlic clove

1 tbsp. sesame oil

½ carrot, sliced

½ onion, chopped

½ cup soy milk

¼ cup flour

⅛ cup tofu, seasoned and crumbled

½ cup water

Directions:

1. Heat the oil on Sauté mode.

2. Add onion and garlic, and stir-fry for 2 minutes or until translucent.

3. Add vegetable broth, half a cup of water, carrots, and broccoli.

4. Seal the lid, press MANUAL, and cook on HIGH for 5 minutes.

5. Once it beeps, perform a quick release, and carefully open the lid.
6. Let cool, then transfer to a food processor. Blend until creamy.
7. Transfer the mixture back into the pot, and add the remaining ingredients.
8. Seal the lid, press MANUAL and cook for 13 more minutes.
9. Once ready, release the pressure naturally for 10 minutes and serve.

Nutritional Info per Serving: Calories 210, Protein 8, Carbs 23, Fat 9

Vichyssoise

(Prep + Cook Time: 20 minutes / Servings: 2)

Ingredients:

½ lb. potatoes, chopped
1 ½ leeks, finely sliced, green part removed
2 ½ fl. oz. silken tofu
2 ½ cups vegetable stock
½ onion, sliced
1 ½ tbsp. butter

1 tsp. lemon juice
⅛ tsp. nutmeg
⅛ tsp. ground coriander
1 small bay leaf
Freshly snipped chives, to garnish

Directions:

1. Melt butter on SAUTÉ, and add the leek and onion.
2. Stir-fry for 5 minutes without browning.
3. Add the vegetable stock, potatoes, nutmeg, lemon juice, coriander, bay leaf, salt and pepper.
4. Lock the lid, press MANUAL, and cook on HIGH pressure for 10 minutes.
5. Once ready, perform a quick pressure release. Carefully open the lid.
6. Remove the bay leaf, and then process the food in a blender until smooth.
7. In a bowl, put the silken tofu and a pinch of salt, mix well.
8. Add a little bit of the soup to this mixture, and then whisk it all back into the soup.
9. Press WARM (or Keep Warm) and reheat, without boiling.
10. Serve chilled, sprinkled with freshly snipped chives.

Nutritional Info per Serving: Calories 115, Protein 1.7, Carbs 11.6, Fat 7.3

Beans Soup with Chili

(Prep + Cook Time: 35 minutes / Servings: 2)

Ingredients:

7 ½ oz. can red kidney beans, rinsed

7 oz. can tomatoes

1 fresh red chilies, finely chopped

1 ½ tbsp. oil

¼ cup tomato pasta sauce

½ clove garlic, crushed

½ green bell pepper, diced

½ tsp. sugar

Directions:

1. Heat oil in Instant Pot, and add garlic, chili, and onion.

2. Stir-fry for 2 minutes, or until translucent.

3. Add the remaining ingredients, and securely lock the lid.

4. Press MANUAL and cook on HIGH pressure for 25 minutes.

5. Once ready, allow for a natural release for 10 minutes.

6. Leave covered for 5 minutes before serving.

Nutritional Info per Serving: Calories 195, Protein 7.3, Carbs 26.5, Fat 7.1

Creamy Beans Soup

(Prep + Cook Time: 20 minutes / Servings: 2)

Ingredients:

2 cups beef broth

½ cup canned beans, cooked

1 potato, chopped

½ tsp. garlic powder

¼ cup heavy cream

Sea salt to taste

½ tsp. ground black pepper

Directions:

1. Add all ingredients and set on MANUAL for 10 minutes.

2. Adjust the steam release and cook on HIGH pressure.

3. Once ready, press Cancel button and release the steam naturally for 10 minutes. Transfer everything to a food processor and blend until smooth.

4. Return the soup to the clean stainless steel insert and add a half cup of water.

5. Cook on SAUTÉ for 5 more minutes. Serve hot and enjoy.

Nutritional Info per Serving: Calories 175, Protein 7.9, Carbs 16.5, Fat 8.8

Pork Soup

(Prep + Cook Time: 55 minutes / Servings: 2)

Ingredients:

2 pork chops, 8 oz., with bones
2 cups beef broth
1 carrot, sliced
1 bay leaf
1 onion, diced

1 celery stalk, diced
1 tsp. oil
½ tsp. chili and garlic powder
½ tbsp. cayenne pepper
1 tbsp. soy sauce

Directions:

1. Press the Sauté button and grease the stainless steel bottom with oil.

2. Add the onion and stir-fry until translucent, for about 2 minutes.

3. Add the celery stalk, carrot, cayenne, and chili pepper. Give it a good stir and continue to cook for 7 - 8 minutes.

4. Press CANCEL and add the add pork chops, garlic powder, bay leaf, and soy sauce. Pour in the broth, and seal the lid. Set the MANUAL mode for 35 minutes on HIGH pressure.

5. Once ready, perform a quick release and open the lid. Let cool for a few minutes and serve.

Nutritional Info per Serving: Calories 331, Protein 30.1, Carbs 14.1, Fat 16.6

Lentils and Tomatoes Soup

(Prep + Cook Time: 15 minutes / Servings: 2)

Ingredients:

2 cups vegetable broth
2 tbsp. tomato paste
1 garlic clove, peeled, crushed
1 cup lentils, soaked overnight, drained
1 tomato, wedged
1 small carrot, thinly sliced

½ tbsp. parsley, chopped
½ small onion, chopped
½ tsp. thyme, dried, ground
1 medium-sized onion, diced
¼ tsp. cumin, ground

Directions:

1. Combine all ingredients in the Instant Pot. Press MANUAL, and cook for 8 minutes on HIGH pressure. Once ready, release the steam naturally for 10 minutes.

2. Carefully open the lid and serve warm.

Nutritional Info per Serving: Calories 326, Protein 35.3, Carbs 26.8, Fat 3.5

Colorful Soup

(Prep + Cook Time: 17 minutes / Servings: 2)

Ingredients:

½ cup wax beans, cut into bite-sized pieces
½ cup green peas
½ small carrot, finely chopped
1 red bell pepper, finely chopped, seeded
½ tomato, diced

1 cup vegetable broth
1 cup water
1 tbsp. olive oil
½ tsp. salt
¼ tsp. oregano, ground, dried

Directions:

1. Combine all ingredients in the Instant Pot. Stir well and seal the lid.

2. Adjust the steam release handle and select MANUAL.

3. Cook on HIGH pressure for 10 minutes.

4. Once ready, release the steam naturally for 10 minutes and serve hot.

Nutritional Info per Serving: Calories 147, Protein 4.5, Carbs 15.3, Fat 8

Fish Soup

(Prep + Cook Time: 45 minutes / Servings: 2)

Ingredients:

3 oz. mackerel fillets
2 cups fish stock
⅛ cup olive oil
¼ cup kidney beans, soaked

¼ cup wheat groats, soaked
⅛ cup sweet corn
¼ lb. tomatoes, peeled and diced
½ tsp. fresh rosemary, chopped

Directions:

1. Grease the bottom of the stainless steel insert of your Instant Pot with olive oil. Press SAUTÉ and add the tomatoes. Cook for 4 minutes, stirring occasionally.

2. Add the corn, rosemary, fish stock, beans, wheat groats and a pinch of salt. Seal the lid.

3. Press MANUAL and set the timer to 30 minutes on HIGH.

4. Once ready, perform a quick release, open the lid, and add the mackerel fillets. Close again and press the STEAM button. Cook for 10 minutes.

Nutritional Info per Serving: Calories 464, Protein 28.3, Carbs 39.1, Fat 21.5

Parsnip Soup

(Prep + Cook Time: 15 minutes / Servings: 2)

Ingredients:

2 cups vegetable stock
½ red onion, finely chopped
2 parsnips, cut into ¾-inch pieces parsnip
1 tbsp. vegetable oil

1 garlic clove, crushed
¼ tsp. chili powder
juice from ½ lemon
Salt and black pepper, to taste

Directions:

1. Heat oil on SAUTÉ. Add the onion, parsnips, and cook for 5 minutes, or until softened.

2. Add the chili powder and garlic, and stir constantly for 1 minute.

3. Stir in the stock and the lemon juice, and securely lock the lid.

4. Select MANUAL and cook on HIGH for 5 minutes. Perform a quick release.

5. Transfer to a food processor and blend for 1 minute to a smooth puree.

6. Return the soup to the pot and WARM for 2 minutes until piping hot.

Nutritional Info per Serving: Calories 110, Protein 1.7, Carbs 11.4, Fat 7.3

Vegetable and Side Dishes

Carrot Beans

(Prep + Cook Time: 20 minutes / Servings: 2)

Ingredients:

1 cup cranberry beans, soaked overnight
½ onion, chopped
1 carrot, chopped
1 tomato, diced

1 tbsp extra virgin olive oil
1 cup of water
fresh parsley

Directions:

1. Press SAUTÉ and heat olive oil. Add the onion and stir-fry for 2-3 minutes, or until translucent. Add the carrots and tomatoes. Stir and cook for 2-3 more minutes.

2. Add the beans, parsley, and water. Stir and seal the lid. Press MANUAL and cook on HIGH pressure for 12 minutes. Once ready, perform a quick release and serve as a side dish.

Nutritional Info per Serving: Calories 310, Protein 15.1, Carbs 32.9, Fat 8.3

Refried Cumin Pinto Beans

(Prep + Cook Time: 60 minutes / Servings: 2)

Ingredients:

1 cup veggie broth
1 cup water
½ tsp. oregano
½ pound dried pinto beans
¼ tsp. black pepper

½ jalapeno, seeded and chopped
½ tsp. cumin
1 tbsp. shortening
¾ cup chopped onion
1 garlic clove, minced

Directions:

1. Place the beans in a bowl and fill it with water. Let soak for 15 minutes. Add all of the remaining ingredients to your Instant Pot.

2. Rinse and drain the beans and add them to your Instant Pot. Seal the lid, select the BEANS/ CHILI mode, and cook for 45 minutes.

3. Once ready, allow pressure to release naturally for 10 minutes. Carefully open the lid and transfer to a blender. Blend with a hand blender.

Nutritional Info per Serving: Calories 236, Protein 13, Carbs 35, Fat 9

Peas with Vegetables

(Prep + Cook Time: 15 minutes / Servings: 2)

Ingredients:

½ cup green peas
½ tomato, chopped
2 tbsp of tomato sauce, canned
1 garlic clove, crushed
½ onion, sliced

1 carrot, sliced
1 potato, chopped
½ celery stalk, chopped
2 cups vegetable stock
1 tbsp olive oil

Directions:

1. Add all ingredients in the Instant Pot and seal the lid.
2. Press MANUAL and cook for 15 minutes on HIGH.
3. Once ready, allow for a natural pressure release for 10 minutes.
4. Carefully open the lid and serve as a side dish to meat or fish.

Nutritional Info per Serving: Calories 231, Protein 6.6, Carbs 37.9, Fat 10.1

Garlicky Green Beans

(Prep + Cook Time: 20 minutes / Servings: 2)

Ingredients:

½ pound green beans
½ cup water
1 ½ tbsp. olive oil

1 garlic clove, minced
1 tbsp. white wine vinegar
1 tbsp. chopped parsley

Directions:

1. Combine the water and green beans in your Instant Pot.
2. Seal the lid, select MANUAL, and cook on HIGH for 1 minute.
3. Perform a quick release and transfer to a serving bowl.
4. In a small bowl, whisk together the olive oil, vinegar, garlic, salt, and pepper.
5. Pour the dressing over the green beans. Toss to combine.
6. Sprinkle with parsley and enjoy.

Nutritional Info per Serving: Calories 143, Protein 3.5, Carbs 9, Fat 11

Potato Stew

(Prep + Cook Time: 35 minutes / Servings: 2)

Ingredients:

2 potatoes, chopped

1 carrot, sliced

2 cups water

2 tbsp olive oil

2 tsp tomato sauce

½ onion, chopped

½ tbsp of celery, chopped

½ tbsp of parsley, chopped

½ chili pepper, sliced

Salt and pepper, to taste

Directions:

1. Heat oil on SAUTÉ mode. Add the onion, carrot, and celery. Stir-fry for 2-3 minutes, or until soft. Do not burn them. Add the water, tomato sauce, and potatoes. Stir and lock the lid. Set to 25 minutes on MANUAL mode at HIGH pressure.

2. Once ready, perform a quick release. Carefully open the lid and add the remaining ingredients. Seal the lid and cook on HIGH for 3 more minutes.

3. Perform a quick pressure release and serve hot.

Nutritional Info per Serving: Calories 316, Protein 4.9, Carbs 42.3, Fat 15.3

Instant Ratatouille

(Prep + Cook Time: 30 minutes / Servings: 2)

Ingredients:

½ tbsp. olive oil

6 oz. canned roasted red peppers, sliced

2 small zucchini, sliced

1 small eggplant, sliced

½ onion, sliced

14 oz. canned crushed tomatoes

Salt to taste

1 garlic clove, minced

¼ cup water

Directions:

1. Set your Instant Pot to SAUTÉ mode and heat the oil.

2. Add all veggies, except for the tomatoes, and sauté for 3 minutes.

3. Pour the water and add the tomatoes. Season with salt.

4. Seal the lid, select MANUAL, and cook on HIGH for 4 minutes.

5. Once ready, release the pressure quickly and serve hot over rice or cold as a side dish.

Nutritional Info per Serving: Calories 232, Protein 4.4, Carbs 40, Fat 4

Quick Yellow Peas

(Prep + Cook Time: 35 minutes / Servings: 2)

Ingredients:

2 cups vegetable stock
1 cup yellow peas, split
1 garlic clove, crushed
1 potato, chopped
1 tbsp butter

½ cup onions, chopped
½ carrot, sliced
½ tsp cayenne pepper
Salt to taste

Directions:

1. Melt butter on SAUTÉ mode and add the onions. Stir-fry for 2 minutes.

2. Add the remaining vegetables and continue to cook for 6-7 minutes.

3. Stir in cayenne pepper and season with salt. Cook for 1 more minute.

4. Pour in the vegetable stock and seal the lid.

5. Set the steam release handle and set to MANUAL for 25 minutes on HIGH.

6. Once ready, perform a quick release and serve.

Nutritional Info per Serving: Calories 316, Protein 9.6, Carbs 36.4, Fat 8.1

Navy Beans with Bacon

(Prep + Cook Time: 60 minutes / Servings: 2)

Ingredients:

½ small onion, chopped
2 oz. bacon, chopped
½ cup navy beans, soaked overnight
¼ tsp. dry mustard

1 oz. dark molasses
¾ cup water
Salt to taste

Directions:

1. Place all of the ingredients into your Instant Pot. Stir to combine.

2. Seal the lid, select MANUAL, and cook on LOW for about 45 minutes.

3. Once ready, release the pressure naturally for 10 minutes.

Nutritional Info per Serving: Calories 190, Protein 7, Carbs 25, Fat 7

Instant Steamed Asparagus

(Prep + Cook Time: 10 minutes / Servings: 2)

Ingredients:

½ pound asparagus spears, trimmed
1 cup water
1 tbsp. olive oil

½ tbsp. diced onion
⅛ tsp. garlic powder
Salt, to taste

Directions:

1. Pour the water into your Instant Pot. Arrange the asparagus on the rack. Drizzle with oil.

2. Sprinkle with diced onion and salt. Seal the lid and set the mode to STEAM.

3. Cook for 2 minutes. Do a quick pressure release. Serve and enjoy!

Nutritional Info per Serving: Calories 84, Protein 2.5, Carbs 4.6, Fat 7.1

Stuffed Eggplant

(Prep + Cook Time: 50 minutes / Servings: 2)

Ingredients:

2 eggplants
½ lb. mushrooms, chopped.
1 cup water
1 cup grated cheddar cheese

½ cup diced celery
½ onion, diced
½ tbsp. olive oil
½ tbsp. dried basil

Directions:

1. Cut the eggplants in half and scoop out the flesh. Save the hollowed out eggplants for later.

2. Pour the water into the pressure cooker. Combine the eggplant filling and the remaining ingredients, except for the cheese.

3. Place the eggplant mixture into the cooking liquid in the Instant Pot and seal the lid. Cook on HIGH pressure for 5 minutes.

4. Once ready, release the pressure naturally, for 10 minutes.

5. Open and divide the filling between the eggplants and arrange them on the rack, drizzle with oil, and sprinkle with salt and pepper.

6. Seal the lid, press MANUAL and cook on HIGH for 15 minutes.

7. Once ready, release the pressure quickly. Sprinkle with the cheese.

8. Return to the pressure cooker and cook for 5 more minutes on HIGH.

Nutritional Info per Serving: Calories 174, Protein 6, Carbs 25, Fat 7

Swiss Chard Omelet

(Prep + Cook Time: 25 minutes / Servings: 2)

Ingredients:

4 eggs, beaten

1 cup Swiss chard, chopped

1 cup water

1 tbsp olive oil

1 cup heavy cream

1 potato, chopped

¼ tsp salt and black pepper

Directions:

1. In a large bowl, combine the eggs, heavy cream, and potato. Sprinkle with salt and pepper, and stir well. Grease the Instant pot with olive oil and press SAUTÉ.

2. Add the Swiss chard. Cook for 5 minutes.

3. Remove the chard from the pot and transfer it to the egg mixture.

4. Add a cup of water to the Instant Pot, and place the egg mixture in a baking dish inside the Instant Pot. Seal the lid.

5. Press MANUAL and cook on LOW pressure for 20 minutes.

6. Once ready, allow for a natural release and serve.

Nutritional Info per Serving: Calories 345, Protein 12.1, Carbs 14.1, Fat 27.2

Bok Choy with Sesame Seeds

(Prep + Cook Time: 5 minutes / Servings: 2)

Ingredients:

½ medium bok choy

1 tsp. sesame seeds

¼ tsp. sesame oil

½ tsp. soy sauce

1 cup water

Directions:

1. Pour the water into your Instant Pot. Lower the basket. Place the bok choy in the steamer basket.

2. Seal the lid, select MANUAL, and cook on HIGH for 4 minutes.

3. Once ready, release the pressure quickly.

4. Chop the bok choy, drizzle with the oil and soy sauce, and sprinkle with sesame seeds.

Nutritional Info per Serving: Calories 54, Protein 3, Carbs 5, Fat 2

Chili Corn on the Cob

(Prep + Cook Time: 10 minutes / Servings: 2)

Ingredients:

1 cup water
½ tbsp. chili powder, divided
2 ears of corn, shucked

2 tsp. butter, divided
Salt and black pepper, to taste

Directions:

1. Pour the water into your Instant Pot.
2. Arrange the ears in the basket.
3. Seal the lid, select MANUAL, and cook on HIGH for 3 minutes.
4. Release the pressure quickly. Top each corn ear with 1 tsp. butter.
5. Sprinkle with chili powder, and season with salt and pepper. Serve hot.

Nutritional Info per Serving: Calories 59, Protein 1.9, Carbs 14.1, Fat 0.5

Spicy Eggplant with Spinach

(Prep + Cook Time: 15 minutes / Servings: 2)

Ingredients:

½ tbsp. five spice powder
1 tbsp. coconut oil
½ cup vegetable stock
¼ cup coconut milk

2 cups cubed eggplant
1 cup torn spinach
½ tsp. chili powder

Directions:

1. Set your Instant Pot to SAUTÉ mode and melt the coconut oil.
2. Place the eggplant cubes, and cook them for 2 minutes, without burning.
3. Add coconut milk and stock, and stir to combine.
4. Stir in the spinach and the seasonings.
5. Seal the lid, select MANUAL, and cook on HIGH for 4 minutes.
6. Once ready, release pressure quickly and serve.

Nutritional Info per Serving: Calories 115, Protein 3, Carbs 8, Fat 6.5

Seasoned Kale with Cashews

(Prep + Cook Time: 10 minutes / Servings: 2)

Ingredients:

½ cup raw cashews
5 oz. kale
1 ½ cups water

¼ cup nutritional yeast
½ tbsp. seasoning, any
1 tsp. vinegar

Directions:

1. Add the kale and pour the water in your Instant Pot.
2. Seal the lid, select MANUAL, and cook on HIGH for 4 minutes.
3. Combine the yeast, cashews, and seasonings, in your food processor.
4. Process until powder forms.
5. Once ready, perform a quick pressure release and transfer the kale to a serving platter and drizzle with vinegar.
6. Top with the yeast and cashew mixture.

Nutritional Info per Serving: Calories 303, Protein 16, Carbs 28, Fat 17

Buttery Rosemary Potatoes

(Prep + Cook Time: 35 minutes / Servings: 2)

Ingredients:

1 ½ tbsp. butter

4 potatoes, sliced

1 cup chicken broth

½ sprig rosemary, chopped

Directions:

1. Set your Instant Pot to SAUTÉ mode and melt the butter.
2. Add potatoes, and cook for 10 minutes, stirring occasionally.
3. Pour in the broth and rosemary, and seal the lid.
4. Select MANUAL, and cook on HIGH for 7 minutes.
5. Once ready, release the pressure quickly and enjoy.

Nutritional Info per Serving: Calories 175, Protein 4, Carbs 27, Fat 4

Lemony Artichokes

(Prep + Cook Time: 40 minutes / Servings: 2)

Ingredients:

2 artichokes

1 ½ cups water

Juice of ½ lemon

½ lemon wedge

1 tbsp. Dijon mustard

Directions:

1. Wash and trim the artichokes, no sharp edges. Rub the top of the artichoke with the lemon wedge. Pour 1.5 cups of water into your Instant Pot.
2. Place the artichoke in the steaming basket, and drizzle with lemon juice.
3. Seal the lid and select MANUAL. Cook on HIGH for 20 minutes.
4. Release the pressure naturally for about 10 minutes. Season the artichokes with salt and pepper, and drizzle with Dijon.

Nutritional Info per Serving: Calories 77, Protein 5.3, Carbs 17, Fat 0.2

Balsamic Wheat Berries with Tomatoes

(Prep + Cook Time: 45 minutes / Servings: 2)

Ingredients:

1 cup wheat berries
7 ½ oz. can diced tomatoes
1 cup chicken broth

Salt and black pepper, to taste
½ tbsp. butter
Balsamic vinegar

Directions:

1. Set your Instant Pot to SAUTÉ and melt the butter. Add wheat berries, and cook for 2 minutes. Stir in tomatoes, chicken broth, and season with salt and pepper.
2. Seal the lid and select MANUAL. Cook on HIGH for 30 minutes.
3. Once ready, release the pressure naturally for 10 minutes.
4. Drizzle with balsamic vinegar.
5. Serve and enjoy!

Nutritional Info per Serving: Calories 130, Protein 3.5, Carbs 14, Fat 7

Poultry

Sticky Chicken Thighs

(Prep + Cook Time: 30 minutes / Servings: 2)

Ingredients:

2 chicken thighs, boneless
2 ½ tbsp. hoisin sauce
1 cup chicken stock
½ tbsp. vinegar

½ tbsp. soy sauce
2 ½ tbsp. chili sauce
2 garlic cloves, minced

Directions:

1. Arrange the chicken at the bottom of the Instant Pot.
2. Whisk together all of the remaining ingredients, in a bowl.
3. Pour this mixture over the chicken thighs.
4. Seal the lid, and select MANUAL. Cook on HIGH for 15 minutes.
5. Once ready, release the pressure naturally for 15 minutes and serve hot.

Nutritional Info per Serving: Calories 416, Protein 29, Carbs 51, Fat 18

Sweet Chicken with Sriracha

(Prep + Cook Time: 15 minutes / Servings: 2)

Ingredients:

1 tsp. sugar
2 chicken breasts, diced
½ tbsp. minced garlic
1 tbsp. cornstarch

1 ½ tbsp. honey
1 ½ tbsp. sriracha
2 ½ tbsp. soy sauce
4 tbsp. water, divided

Directions:

1. Combine 1 tbsp. water, soy sauce, sriracha, honey, garlic, and sugar in your Instant Pot. Add the chicken and stir. Seal the lid, select MANUAL, and cook on HIGH for 9 minutes.
2. Open the lid, whisk together the cornstarch and remaining water.
3. Stir into the chicken and cook for another 3 minutes on SAUTÉ mode.

Nutritional Info per Serving: Calories 419, Protein 67, Carbs 19, Fat 7

Chicken Alfredo with Cauliflower

(Prep + Cook Time: 30 minutes / Servings: 2)

Ingredients:

2 chicken breasts, boneless and skinless, chopped
2 basil leaves, chopped
2 garlic cloves, chopped

1 cup heavy cream
4 oz. cream cheese
¼ cup of butter
1 cup cauliflower florets

Directions:

1. Set your Instant Pot to SAUTÉ mode.
2. Melt the butter, and whisk in the cream cheese.
3. While whisking, add the heavy cream.
4. Stir in the remaining ingredients.
5. Seal the lid, select MANUAL, and cook on HIGH for 15 minutes.
6. Once ready, release the pressure quickly and serve immediately.

Nutritional Info per Serving: Calories 325, Protein 22, Carbs 7, Fat 18

Buffalo Chicken and Potatoes

(Prep + Cook Time: 35 minutes / Servings: 2)

Ingredients:

½ onion, diced
1 ½ tbsp. buffalo wing sauce
¼ tsp. garlic powder
8 oz. potatoes, diced

1 cup chicken broth
½ lb. chicken breasts, cut into cubes
1 ½ tbsp. butter, divided
Salt and black pepper, to taste

Directions:

1. Melt ½ tbsp. the butter in your Instant Pot on SAUTÉ mode.
2. Add the onions, and cook for 4 minutes, until translucent.
3. Stir in the remaining ingredients, seal the lid, and select POULTRY.
4. Cook for 18 minutes. Once ready, do a quick release and serve hot.

Nutritional Info per Serving: Calories 290, Protein 20, Carbs 25, Fat 12

Honey and Ketchup Chicken

(Prep + Cook Time: 45 minutes / Servings: 2)

Ingredients:

1 ½ tbsp. ketchup
⅛ cup honey
2 chicken thighs, boneless
Salt and black pepper, to taste

1 tsp. garlic powder
⅛ cup butter
⅛ cup coconut aminos

Directions:

1. Place everything in your Instant Pot. Stir well to combine.

2. Seal the lid, and select MANUAL. Cook on HIGH for 18 minutes.

3. When ready, perform a quick pressure release.

4. Set it to SAUTÉ and cook for 5 more minutes until well cooked.

Nutritional Info per Serving: Calories 457, Protein 44, Carbs 21, Fat 20

Cream Cheese and Bacon Chicken

(Prep + Cook Time: 40 minutes / Servings: 2)

Ingredients:

1 cup water
4 oz. cream cheese
1 lb. chicken breasts, boneless and skinless
2 oz. cheddar cheese, shredded

½ ounce ranch seasoning
4 bacon slices, cooked and crumbled
1 ½ tbsp. cornstarch

Directions:

1. Combine the water, cream cheese, and ranch seasoning in your Instant Pot.

2. Add the chicken, and seal the lid.

3. Select MANUAL, and cook on HIGH for 25 minutes.

4. Do a quick release, transfer the chicken to a plate, and shred it.

5. Return the shredded chicken to the pot along with the cheddar and bacon.

6. Cook on SAUTÉ mode for 5 minutes, without the lid.

7. Stir in cornstarch, and cook for a few more minutes, until sauce is thickened.

Nutritional Info per Serving: Calories 611, Protein 58, Carbs 13, Fat 42

Lemon Garlic Chicken

(Prep + Cook Time: 25 minutes / Servings: 2)

Ingredients:

½ onion, diced
2 garlic cloves, minced
1 tbsp. white wine
⅛ tsp. paprika
1 lb. chicken breasts, chopped

Juice of ½ lemon
½ tbsp. butter
1 ½ tsp. flour
¼ cup broth

Directions:

1. Melt the butter in your Instant Pot on SAUTÉ mode.

2. Add the onions, and cook for 3 minutes. Add garlic, and cook for 1 minute.

3. Stir in all of the remaining ingredients, except for the flour.

4. Seal the lid, and cook on POULTRY at default time.

5. Release the pressure quickly. Stir in the flour, and cook on SAUTÉ until it thickens. Serve and enjoy.

Nutritional Info per Serving: Calories 530, Protein 65, Carbs 5, Fat 23

Sour Cream and Tomato Chicken

(Prep + Cook Time: 45 minutes / Servings: 2)

Ingredients:

2 chicken breasts, boneless
½ cup sour cream
7 oz. can tomatoes, diced

⅛ tsp. garlic powder
Salt and black pepper, to taste
1 cup chicken broth

Directions:

1. Combine the chicken and broth in your Instant Pot.

2. Seal the lid, and select MANUAL. Cook on HIGH for 20 minutes.

3. Do a quick release and transfer the chicken to a plate. Shred it. Discard the excess cooking liquid. Set the Instant Pot to SAUTÉ mode.

4. Stir in all of the remaining ingredients, including the shredded chicken.

5. Cook for 5 minutes. Serve and enjoy!

Nutritional Info per Serving: Calories 254, Protein 30, Carbs 6, Fat 20

Chicken Thighs with Potatoes

(Prep + Cook Time: 10 minutes / Servings: 2)

Ingredients:

2 boneless chicken thighs
2 potatoes, wedged
1 garlic clove, crushed
½ tbsp. lemon juice
1 cup water

¼ tbsp. cayenne pepper
½ tsp. fresh mint, chopped
½ tsp. ground ginger
⅛ cup olive oil
Salt to taste

Directions:

1. In a small bowl, add the olive oil, lemon juice, crushed garlic, ground ginger, mint, cayenne pepper, and a pinch of salt. Brush each chicken piece with the mixture.
2. Grease the Instant Pot with the remaining mixture. Place the potatoes into the pot and place the chicken. Add water and seal the lid. Press MEAT and cook for 15 minutes.
3. Once ready, release the steam naturally for 10 minutes and serve hot.

Nutritional Info per Serving: Calories 414, Protein 34.8, Carbs 35.1, Fat 11.6

Chicken Wings in Yogurt Sauce

(Prep + Cook Time: 35 minutes / Servings: 2)

Ingredients:

1 lb. chicken wings
1 cup chicken broth

1 tbsp. of olive oil
½ tsp. of salt

For the yogurt sauce:

½ cup of yogurt
¼ cup of sour cream

1 garlic clove, crushed

Directions:

1. Press the SAUTÉ and heat the olive oil. Place the wings and brown them for 8 minutes, flipping once. Add the chicken broth, press MEAT and set to 15 minutes. Once ready, allow for a natural release, for 10 minutes.
2. For the sauce, combine the sour cream with yogurt and garlic, in a bowl.
3. Let the wings cool for a while and top with the yogurt mixture before serving.

Nutritional Info per Serving: Calories 438, Protein 36.8, Carbs 15.3, Fat 21.3

Simple Leftover Chicken with Broccoli

(Prep + Cook Time: 15 minutes / Servings: 2)

Ingredients:

1 ½ cups shredded leftover chicken
1 cup broccoli florets
¼ cup heavy cream

¼ cup grated Parmesan cheese
½ cup chicken broth
Salt and black pepper, to taste

Directions:

1. Place the chicken, broccoli, and broth into your Instant Pot.
2. Seal the lid, select MANUAL, and cook for 2 minutes on HIGH.
3. When ready, release the pressure quickly.
4. Carefully open the lid and stir in all of the remaining ingredients.
5. Set it to SAUTÉ and cook for 1 minute. Serve immediately.

Nutritional Info per Serving: Calories 354, Protein 33, Carbs 4, Fat 24

Lemon Chicken Legs

(Prep + Cook Time: 60 minutes / Servings: 2)

Ingredients:

2 chicken legs
¼ cup white wine
1 tbsp. triple sec
¼ cup chopped celery
1 tbsp. chopped parsley
1 tbsp. vinegar

Juice and zest of ½ lemon
1 garlic clove, chopped
¼ cup chopped shallots
¼ cup chopped carrots
½ tbsp. oil
Salt and black pepper, to taste

Directions:

1. Heat the oil in your Instant Pot on SAUTÉ mode.
2. Place the legs inside and brown them on all sides, for about 4 -5 minutes.
3. Transfer them to a plate. Add the remaining ingredients, and stir to combine.
4. Return the legs to the pot. Seal the lid, select MANUAL, and cook on HIGH for 45 minutes. When ready, release the pressure quickly and serve immediately.

Nutritional Info per Serving: Calories 530, Protein 35, Carbs 34, Fat 31

Chicken with Herbs

(Prep + Cook Time: 10 minutes / Servings: 2)

Ingredients:

2 chicken thighs
1 ½ cup chicken broth
1 garlic clove, crushed
½ cup extra virgin olive oil, divided
1 tbsp. lemon juice

½ tbsp. fresh basil, thyme and rosemary, chopped
½ tsp. cayenne pepper
½ tsp. salt
⅛ cup apple cider vinegar

Directions:

1. In a large bowl, combine olive oil, lemon juice, apple cider, garlic, vinegar, basil, rosemary, thyme, salt, and cayenne pepper.

2. Douse the thighs into this mixture, and refrigerate for 1 hour.

3. Remove the meat from the refrigerator, and pat dry using paper towel.

4. Pour the chicken broth into the Instant Pot.

5. Set the steamer insert, and place the chicken in it.

6. Seal the lid, press STEAM and cook for 15 minutes.

7. Do a natural release for 10 minutes and remove the chicken and the broth.

8. Grease with oil, add back the chicken and press SAUTÉ.

9. Brown for 5 minutes, flipping the thighs once.

Nutritional Info per Serving: Calories 359, Protein 37.3, Carbs 12.3, Fat 16.3

Mushrooms and Chicken Thighs

(Prep + Cook Time: 30 minutes / Servings: 2)

Ingredients:

2 chicken thighs
6 oz. button mushrooms
2 tbsp. olive oil, divided
1 garlic cloves, crushed

½ tbsp. Italian seasoning mix
½ tbsp. butter
½ tsp. salt
½ tsp. fresh rosemary, finely chopped

Directions:

1. Rub the meat with salt. Grease the Instant Pot with 1 tbsp. of oil.

2. Add the chicken thighs and 3 cups of water.

3. Press MEAT and cook for 15 minutes.

4. Once ready, perform a quick release and open the lid.

5. Remove the thighs, drain and set aside.

6. Grease the steel insert with 1 tbsp. of oil, and add mushrooms, rosemary, and Italian seasoning mix.

7. Press SAUTÉ, and cook for 5 minutes, stirring constantly.

8. Add and melt the butter. Then add the chicken thighs, and gently brown them on all sides.

9. Serve immediately.

Nutritional Info per Serving: Calories 431, Protein 42.5, Carbs 13.6, Fat 13

Creamy Chicken

(Prep + Cook Time: 30 minutes / Servings: 2)

Ingredients:

1 lb. boneless chicken, cut into pieces

½ onion, diced

½ tsp. turmeric

½ tsp. paprika

½ tsp. coriander

½ bell pepper, diced

1 garlic clove, minced

½ cup coconut cream

7 oz. tomato sauce

1 tbsp. butter

Directions:

1. Set your Instant Pot to SAUTÉ mode and melt the butter.

2. Stir in onion and bell pepper, and cook for 3 minutes.

3. Add garlic, and cook for 1 minute.

4. Place the chicken and brown for 2 minutes.

5. Stir in the remaining ingredients, except for the coconut cream.

6. Seal the lid, and select POULTRY. Cook for 15 minutes.

7. Release the pressure naturally, for 5 minutes and stir in the coconut cream.

8. Give it a good stir and serve immediately.

Nutritional Info per Serving: Calories 483, Protein 36, Carbs 17, Fat 21

Shredded Turkey with Mustard and Beer

(Prep + Cook Time: 65 minutes / Servings: 2)

Ingredients:

6 oz. dark beer

½ tbsp. mustard

1 turkey thigh

¼ tsp. pepper

turkey thighs tbsp. tomato paste

turkey thighs tsp. dry mustard

¼ tsp. garlic powder

1 tbsp. apple cider vinegar

1 tbsp. brown sugar

1 tsp. coriander

Directions:

1. Mix the seasonings, all except the beer and the turkey, in a small bowl. Rub the seasoning onto the turkey. Pour the beer in the Instant Pot, and add the turkey. Seal the lid, select MANUAL, and cook on HIGH for 45 minutes.

2. Once ready, do a quick release. Transfer the turkey to a plate and shred it. Whisk in the remaining ingredients, and bring the mixture to a boil on SAUTÉ mode. Stir in the shredded turkey. Cook for 3 minutes and serve hot.

Nutritional Info per Serving: Calories 515, Protein 51, Carbs 17, Fat 19

Creamy Turkey with Mushrooms

(Prep + Cook Time: 5 minutes / Servings: 2)

Ingredients:

1 lb. turkey breasts

3 oz. mushrooms, sliced

1 tbsp. olive oil

½ tsp. thyme

⅓ cup white wine

1 garlic clove, minced

1 ½ tbsp. heavy cream

1 ½ tbsp. chopped shallots

½ tbsp. cornstarch

⅓ cup chicken broth

Directions:

1. Tie the turkey crosswise, about every 2 inches, with kitchen twine.

2. Heat the oil in the Instant Pot on SAUTÉ, and brown the turkey on all sides.

3. Transfer to a plate. In the Instant Pot, add the mushrooms, shallots, thyme, garlic, and cook for a few minutes, until soft. Then add the turkey and pour in the broth and white wine.

4. Seal the lid, select MANUAL, and cook on HIGH for 15 minutes.

5. When ready, do a quick release and set the Pot to SAUTÉ. Transfer the turkey to a plate, untie and slice.

6. In the pot, whisk in the heavy cream and cornstarch. Cook until thickened. Serve with sauce.

Nutritional Info per Serving: Calories 192, Protein 15, Carbs 5, Fat 7

Simple Turkey Patties

(Prep + Cook Time: 30 minutes / Servings: 2)

Ingredients:

½ lb. ground turkey
½ tbsp. olive oil
⅛ cup breadcrumbs
1 egg

½ tbsp. chopped parsley
⅛ tsp. garlic powder
1 cup chicken broth
Salt and black pepper, to taste

Directions:

1. Combine the turkey, parsley, breadcrumbs, garlic powder, egg, salt, and pepper, in a bowl. Make 2 patties out of the mixture. Heat the oil in your Instant Pot on SAUTÉ mode.

2. Add the patties and cook until browned on all sides. Transfer to a plate.

3. Pour the broth inside the Instant Pot, and arrange the patties on the rack.

4. Seal the lid, select MANUAL, and cook for 5 minutes on HIGH.

5. When ready, release the pressure quickly. Serve and enjoy!

Nutritional Info per Serving: Calories 254, Protein 25.6, Carbs 5.1, Fat 17.3

Turkey Verde Casserole

(Prep + Cook Time: 35 minutes / Servings: 4)

Ingredients:

1 lb. turkey tenderloins
1 cup chicken broth
½ cup brown rice

½ onion, sliced
¼ cup salsa verde
Salt to taste

Directions:

1. Combine all of the ingredients in your Instant Pot. Seal the lid, and select MANUAL.

2. Cook on HIGH for 8 minutes. When ready, release the pressure naturally for 10 minutes.

Nutritional Info per Serving: Calories 421, Protein 35.5, Carbs 47, Fat 4.1

Turkey Burgers

(Prep + Cook Time: 15 minutes / Servings: 2)

Ingredients:

½ lb. ground turkey

½ cup sour cream

1 egg

½ cup all-purpose flour

½ small onion, chopped

½ tsp. dried dill, chopped

Directions:

1. Combine all ingredients in a large mixing bowl. Mix with hands and set aside.
2. Form patties with the previously prepared mixture.
3. Line parchment paper on a baking dish that fits in the Instant Pot Mini, and place the patties. Insert it in the Instant Pot and seal the lid.
4. Adjust the steam release handle and press MANUAL. Cook on HIGH pressure for 12 minutes. When ready, release the steam naturally, for about 5 minutes.
5. Serve with lettuce and tomatoes.

Nutritional Info per Serving: Calories 345, Protein 27.3, Carbs 19.5, Fat 18.5

Quick Turkey Casserole

(Prep + Cook Time: 20 minutes / Servings: 2)

Ingredients:

1 cup cooked and shredded turkey

½ zucchini, shredded

½ cup sour cream

½ cup cooked rice

½ cup halved cherry tomatoes

¼ cup kalamata olives, chopped

¼ cup chicken broth

1 tbsp. diced onion

1 garlic clove, minced

½ tbsp. butter

Directions:

1. Set your Instant Pot to SAUTÉ mode. Stir in the onions and cook them for 2 minutes, until translucent. Add the garlic, and cook it for 1 minute or until fragrant.
2. Stir in the remaining ingredients and seal the lid.
3. Press MANUAL mode and cook on HIGH pressure for 3 minutes.
4. When ready, release the pressure quickly and serve hot.

Nutritional Info per Serving: Calories 454, Protein 19, Carbs 16, Fat 14

Seasoned Turkey Drumsticks

(Prep + Cook Time: 5 minutes / Servings: 2)

Ingredients:

3 turkey drumsticks
¼ cup water
½ tsp. black pepper

1 tsp. brown sugar
¼ cup soy sauce
¼ tsp. garlic powder

Directions:

1. Combine all of the spices together, and rub this mixture onto the turkey.
2. Whisk together the water and soy sauce in your Instant Pot.
3. Then add the drumsticks, and seal the lid.
4. Select MANUAL, and cook on HIGH pressure for 25 minutes.
5. When ready, release the pressure quickly and serve immediately.

Nutritional Info per Serving: Calories 205, Protein 24, Carbs 4, Fat 3

Easy Turkey in Tomato Sauce

(Prep + Cook Time: 30 minutes / Servings: 2)

Ingredients:

½ lb. ground turkey
14 oz. can diced tomatoes
½ tsp. Italian seasoning
½ tsp. garlic powder
⅛ cup breadcrumbs
½ tsp. dried basil

⅛ cup chicken stock
½ tsp. dried oregano
v tsp. dried thyme
1 tbsp. onion, diced
Salt and black pepper, to taste

Directions:

1. Combine the turkey, basil, oregano, thyme, breadcrumbs, salt, and pepper, in a large bowl.
2. Make meatballs out of the mixture.
3. In your Instant Pot, combine the remaining ingredients.
4. Place the meatballs inside the Instant Pot and select MANUAL mode.
5. Cook on HIGH pressure for 10 minutes.
6. When ready, perform a quick pressure quickly and serve immediately.

Nutritional Info per Serving: Calories 322, Protein 27, Carbs 5, Fat 14

Beef and Pork

Instant Beef Bourguignon

(Prep + Cook Time: 75 minutes / Servings: 2)

Ingredients:

½ cup red wine
½ red onion, chopped
½ tbsp. maple syrup
¼ lb. bacon, cut into small pieces
½ lb. beef, cut into cubes
¼ cup beef broth

1 garlic clove, minced
½ tbsp. oil
2 carrots, peeled and sliced
1 sweet potato, peeled and cubed
Salt and black pepper, to taste

Directions:

1. Set your Instant Pot to Sauté mode and heat the oil. Stir in the onions and cook for 3 minutes. Add garlic, and cook for 1 minute. Add beef, and cook for about 5 minutes per side.

2. Stir in the bacon and cook for 1 minute. Stir in the remaining ingredients. Set the Pot to MANUAL, and cook on HIGH for 30 minutes. Once ready, release the pressure naturally.

Nutritional Info per Serving: Calories 566, Protein 55, Carbs 35, Fat 37

Sweet Short Ribs

(Prep + Cook Time: 4 hours and 40 minutes / Servings: 2)

Ingredients:

½ cup water
Juice of ½ orange
1 garlic clove, crushed
¼ tbsp. sesame oil

2 beef short ribs
¼ cup brown sugar
⅓ cup soy sauce
½ tsp. grated ginger

Directions:

1. Whisk together all of the ingredients, except the ribs, in a bowl. Add the ribs, cover the bowl, and store the marinade in the fridge for 4 hours.

2. Then, transfer the beef to the Instant Pot along with the marinade. Seal the lid, and select MANUAL. Cook on HIGH pressure for 30 minutes. Once ready, release the pressure naturally for 10 minutes and serve hot.

Nutritional Info per Serving: Calories 561, Protein 43, Carbs 76, Fat 10

Instant Pastrami

(Prep + Cook Time: 5 minutes / Servings: 2)

Ingredients:

¼ tbsp. onion powder
¼ tbsp. brown sugar
¼ tbsp. garlic powder
½ tsp. paprika

⅛ tsp. ground cloves
1 lb. corned beef
1 cup water
1 tbsp. vegetable oil

Directions:

1. Pour the water into your Instant Pot. Lower the trivet, and add the beef.

2. Select MANUAL, and cook on HIGH for 45 minutes.

3. Once ready, release the pressure naturally for 10 minutes.

4. Coat the meat with oil, and rub the spices onto it.

5. Set the Instant Pot to SAUTÉ, and cook the meat for about a minute per side. Serve immediately.

Nutritional Info per Serving: Calories 113, Protein 11, Carbs 5, Fat 3.5

Chili Paleo Meatballs

(Prep + Cook Time: 35 minutes / Servings: 2)

Ingredients:

½ lb. ground beef
⅛ cup arrowroot
½ tsp. garlic salt
¼ tsp. paprika

¼ cup chili sauce
2 tbsp. grape jelly
1 egg

Directions:

1. Combine the meat, arrowroot, garlic salt, and egg, in a bowl.

2. Make meatballs out of the mixture. In your Instant Pot, whisk together the remaining ingredients.

3. Add the meatballs to the Instant Pot. Seal the lid, and cook on MANUAL on LOW pressure for 30 minutes.

4. Once ready, release the pressure quickly. Serve and enjoy!

Nutritional Info per Serving: Calories 583, Protein 51, Carbs 26, Fat 19

Pork Goulash

(Prep + Cook Time: 35 minutes / Servings: 2)

Ingredients:

¼ lb. pork neck, cut into pieces
¼ lb. mushrooms
2 tbsp. vegetable oil
2 cups beef broth
½ small chili pepper, sliced

1 onion, chopped
½ medium-sized carrot
½ tbsp. cayenne
½ stalk chopped celery

Directions:

1. Grease the Instant Pot with oil, and press the SAUTÉ button.

2. Add onion, and fry for 2 minutes, until translucent.

3. Add chili powder, carrot, celery, cayenne, and cook for 3 more minutes, stirring constantly.

4. Press CANCEL, add the meat, mushrooms and beef broth.

5. Set on MANUAL and cook for 30 minutes.

6. When ready, perform a quick release and serve warm.

Nutritional Info per Serving: Calories 413, Protein 37, Carbs 16.3, Fat 21.6

New Mexico Chili Pork

(Prep + Cook Time: 55 minutes / Servings: 2)

Ingredients:

½ lb. pork shoulder
3 New Mexico chilies, halved, seeded
1 ½ cup beef broth

1 garlic clove, crushed
½ tsp. ground cumin
½ onion, chopped

Directions:

1. In a small saucepan, toss the chilies, and add garlic and onion.

2. Pour 1 ½ cups of water into the saucepan and bring to a boil.

3. Once boiled, let it cool for 10-15 minutes.

4. Take the mixture from the saucepan and process in a blender until smooth.

5. Place the pork into the Instant Pot. Add in the beef broth and the pureed mixture. Press the MEAT button and cook for 30 minutes.

6. Once done, release the pressure naturally for 10 minutes.

Nutritional Info per Serving: Calories 401, Protein 33.7, Carbs 10.1, Fat 26.3

Round Steak with Vegetables

(Prep + Cook Time: 40 minutes / Servings: 2)

Ingredients:

½ lb. round steak, cubed
2 bell peppers, chopped
½ cup of mushroom slices
2 potatoes, cubed
1 carrot, peeled and chopped

1 tbsp. butter
1 tbsp. flour
½ tsp. garlic salt
¼ tsp. onion powder
1 cup beef broth

Directions:

1. Combine the steak and flour.
2. Set your Instant Pot to SAUTÉ mode and melt the butter.
3. Place the meat and cook until browned on all sides, for a few minutes.
4. Add the veggies, seasoning, and broth to the pot.
5. Seal the lid, and cook on the MEAT/STEW mode for 35 minutes.
6. Do a quick pressure release and drain the excess liquid before serving.

Nutritional Info per Serving: Calories 308, Protein 35, Carbs 21, Fat 8.5

Pork Tenderloin

(Prep + Cook Time: 55 minutes / Servings: 2)

Ingredients:

1 lb. pork tenderloin
2 tbsp. brown sugar
2 tbsp. balsamic vinegar
1 tbsp. butter

1 garlic clove, crushed
½ cup beef broth
Salt and black pepper

Directions:

1. Melt butter on SAUTÉ mode and add garlic. Fry for 1-2 minutes.
2. Add sugar and vinegar, and cook for another minute.
3. Place the meat in the Instant Pot and pour in beef broth.
4. Select MANUAL and cook for 35 minutes on HIGH pressure.
5. When done, perform a quick release and serve.

Nutritional Info per Serving: Calories 426, Protein 42.5, Carbs 17.3, Fat 18.6

Maple Pork Chops

(Prep + Cook Time: 50 minutes / Servings: 2)

Ingredients:

1 lb. pork chops
¼ cup maple syrup
1 tbsp. Dijon mustard
¼ cup beef broth

½ tsp. ginger, grated
¼ tsp. cinnamon
Salt and black pepper to taste

Directions:

1. Season the chops with salt and pepper. Place them in the Pot and press SAUTÉ. Cook for 3-4 minutes or until browned on each side.

2. In a bowl, mix well maple syrup, mustard, cinnamon and ginger. Sprinkle the mixture over the chops and pour in the beef broth. Seal the lid, select MANUAL and cook for 30 minutes.

3. When ready, perform a quick release and serve.

Nutritional Info per Serving: Calories 556, Protein 37.3, Carbs 21.3, Fat 39.1

Worcestershire and Vinegar Flank Steak

(Prep + Cook Time: 25 minutes / Servings: 2)

Ingredients:

1 lb. steak
1 tbsp. vinegar (preferably apple cider)
½ tbsp. Worcestershire sauce

¼ cup oil
1 tbsp. onion soup mix

Directions:

1. Set your Instant Pot to SAUTÉ mode and heat the olive oil.

2. Add the steak and cook until it brown, for about 2-3 minutes per side.

3. Stir in the remaining ingredients.

4. Seal the lid, and select MANUAL mode.

5. Cook on HIGH for 25 minutes. When ready, do a quick pressure release.

6. Serve immediately.

Nutritional Info per Serving: Calories 593, Protein 56, Carbs 5, Fat 44

Cranberry and Cinnamon Pork Roast

(Prep + Cook Time: 85 minutes / Servings: 2)

Ingredients:

5 oz. bone broth
1 tbsp. chopped herbs
6 oz. fresh cranberries
1 lb. pork roast
1 tbsp. apple cider vinegar

½ tbsp. honey
½ tbsp. butter
¼ tsp. cinnamon
⅛ tsp. garlic powder

Directions:

1. Set the Instant Pot to SAUTÉ mode.
2. Melt the butter, and brown the pork on all sides.
3. Stir in the remaining ingredients. Seal the lid, and select MANUAL mode.
4. Cook on HIGH pressure for 70 minutes.
5. When ready, release the pressure naturally, for 10 minutes and serve hot.

Nutritional Info per Serving: Calories 623, Protein 48, Carbs 30, Fat 38

Braised Pork Loin in Milk

(Prep + Cook Time: 55 minutes / Servings: 2)

Ingredients:

1 bay leaf
2 cups milk
½ tsp. salt

½ tsp. black pepper
1 tbsp. olive oil
1 lb. pork loin

Directions:

1. Set the Instant Pot to SAUTÉ. Heat the oil, and brown the pork on all sides.
2. Season with salt and pepper. Add the milk and bay leaf.
3. Seal the lid, and select MANUAL.
4. Cook on HIGH pressure for 30 minutes.
5. Wait 10 minutes before releasing the pressure quickly. Serve immediately.

Nutritional Info per Serving: Calories 380, Protein 45, Carbs 4, Fat 19

Creamy Pork Sausage

(Prep + Cook Time: 35 minutes / Servings: 2)

Ingredients:

½ lb. pork sausage
1 garlic clove, minced
cooking spray for greasing

¼ cup flour
1 cup milk, divided

Directions:

1. Grease the Instant Pot with cooking spray, and set it to SAUTÉ mode.

2. Add garlic, and cook for 1 minute.

3. Add sausage, and cook until brown, breaking it with a spatula as it cooks. Pour in ½ cup of milk. Seal the lid and select MANUAL mode. Cook on HIGH for 5 minutes.

4. Release the pressure quickly. Whisk together the remaining milk and flour.

5. Set on SAUTÉ mode and pour this mixture over the sausage. Cook for 5 minutes.

6. Serve immediately and enjoy.

Nutritional Info per Serving: Calories 487, Protein 28, Carbs 17, Fat 32

Sweet Mustard Pork Chops

(Prep + Cook Time: 25 minutes / Servings: 2)

Ingredients:

1 lb. pork chops
1 tbsp. Dijon mustard
⅛ cup honey
⅛ tsp. black pepper

¼ tsp. cinnamon
¼ tbsp. maple syrup
¼ tsp. grated ginger
Salt to taste

Directions:

1. Season the pork chops with salt and pepper.

2. In a big bowl, whisk together the remaining ingredients.

3. Rub and massage the pork chops onto this mixture and refrigerate for 20 minutes.

4. Transfer the marinated pork chops to the Instant Pot.

5. Add a few tablespoons of water if the marinade is too thick.

6. Seal the lid, select MANUAL. Cook on HIGH pressure for 15 minutes.

7. When ready, release the pressure quickly. Serve immediately with green salad or rice.

Nutritional Info per Serving: Calories 567, Protein 36, Carbs 23, Fat 32

Pork in Creamy Mushroom Sauce

(Prep + Cook Time: 35 minutes / Servings: 2)

Ingredients:

½ can cream of mushroom soup   1 cup water
2 pork chops   1 tbsp. oil

Directions:

1. Heat the oil in your Instant Pot on SAUTÉ mode.
2. Add pork, and cook until browned on all sides. Transfer to a platter.
3. Pour water into the pot and deglaze it.
4. Return the pork, and pour the mushroom soup over the chops.
5. Seal the lid, select MANUAL mode and cook on HIGH for 18 minutes.
6. When ready, release the pressure naturally, about 10 minutes and serve.

Nutritional Info per Serving: Calories 363, Protein 21, Carbs 1, Fat 32

Stews and Chilies

Red Bean and Plantain Stew

(Prep + Cook Time: 80 minutes / Servings: 2)

Ingredients:

1 carrot, chopped
½ plantain, chopped
½ tomato, chopped
¼ lb. dry red beans
½ onion, chopped

1 tbsp. oil
½ green onion, sliced
Water, as needed
Salt and pepper, to taste

Directions:

1. Set your Instant Pot to SAUTÉ mode. Heat the oil, and sauté the onions for 3 minutes.

2. Add the beans and pour enough water to cover. Close the Instant Pot, select MANUAL, and cook on HIGH for 30 minutes.

3. When ready, release the pressure naturally for 10 minutes. Carefully open the lid and stir in the remaining ingredients. Seal the lid, and cook on HIGH pressure for another 30 minutes.

4. Once ready, do a natural pressure release, for 10 minutes. Serve and enjoy!

Nutritional Info per Serving: Calories 110, Protein 4, Carbs 13, Fat 3

Spicy Chicken Curry

(Prep + Cook Time: 35 minutes / Servings: 2)

Ingredients:

½ can corn, undrained
½ can diced tomatoes, undrained
½ tbsp. curry powder
1 tsp. cumin

1 tsp. chili powder
½ can beans, drained
½ lb. chicken breasts, cut into chunks
1 cup chicken broth

Directions:

1. Place all ingredients into your Instant Pot and stir to combine well. Seal the lid, select MANUAL mode and cook on High pressure for 20 minutes.

2. When ready, release the pressure naturally, about 10 minutes. Open the lid and shred the chicken with two forks, inside the Instant Pot. Serve and enjoy!

Nutritional Info per Serving: Calories 487, Protein 32, Carbs, Fat 7

Cheesy Buffalo Chicken Stew

(Prep + Cook Time: 20 minutes / Servings: 2)

Ingredients:

¼ cup diced onion

1 tbsp. butter

½ tbsp. ranch dressing mix

1 garlic clove, minced

¼ cup diced celery

1 cup grated cheddar cheese

1 chicken breast, boneless and skinless

1 cup chicken broth

½ cup heavy cream

¼ cup hot sauce

Directions:

1. Place everything, except the cream and cheddar into the Instant Pot.

2. Seal the lid and select MANUAL mode. Cook on HIGH pressure for 15 minutes.

3. When ready, release the pressure naturally for 10 minutes.

4. Carefully open the lid and shred the chicken inside the Instant Pot.

5. Stir in the cream and cheese and serve.

Nutritional Info per Serving: Calories 528, Protein 35, Carbs 4.1, Fat 40.9

Classic Beef Stew

(Prep + Cook Time: 35 minutes / Servings: 2)

Ingredients:

½ lb. beef, cut into chunks

1 sweet potato, cut into chunks

¼ cup red wine

1 ½ cup beef broth

2 oz. baby carrots, sliced

2 oz. tomato paste

½ onion, chopped

¼ cup green peas

½ tbsp. bacon grease

1 garlic clove, crushed

½ tsp. thyme, dried

1 bay leaf

Directions:

1. Grease the bottom of the Instant Pot with bacon grease. Place the beef and cook on SAUTÉ mode or 10 minutes. Add the onion and garlic.

2. Continue to cook for 5 more minutes, stirring constantly. Add the remaining ingredients and seal the lid. Press MEAT and adjust the cooking time to 20 minutes.

3. When done, perform a quick release and serve hot.

Nutritional Info per Serving: Calories 428, Protein 46.3, Carbs 21.5, Fat 14.5

Veggie Tarragon Stew

(Prep + Cook Time: 25 minutes / Servings: 2)

Ingredients:

½ onion, diced
1 cup chopped parsnips
1 carrot, peeled and chopped
2 tomatoes, chopped
½ tbsp. chopped tarragon
1 tbsp. olive oil

1 garlic clove, minced
2 cups veggie stock
1 cup cubed red potatoes
½ cup chopped red bell peppers
½ cup cubed beets
Salt and black pepper, to taste

Directions:

1. Set your Instant Pot to SAUTÉ mode and heat the olive oil.

2. Add the garlic and onion, and stir-fry 2-3 minutes. Add the other veggies, and continue to cook for 3 minutes.

3. Pour the broth in, and season with salt and pepper. Seal the lid and select the MANUAL mode. Cook on HIGH pressure for 7 minutes.

4. Once ready, release the pressure naturally for 10 minutes and serve hot.

Nutritional Info per Serving: Calories 354, Protein 13, Carbs 38, Fat 12

Zucchini Stew

(Prep + Cook Time: 20 minutes / Servings: 4)

Ingredients:

2 zucchinis, peeled and sliced
1 red bell pepper
½ eggplant, peeled and sliced
¼ cup water

1 tbsp of olive oil
¼ cup tomato juice
½ tsp of Italian seasoning

Directions:

1. Grease the bottom of the stainless steel insert with the olive oil.

2. Add the zucchini, eggplant, pepper, tomato juice, Italian seasoning, salt, and ¼ cup of water, stir well. Seal the lid, press MANUAL and cook on HIGH pressure for 15 minutes.

3. Once ready, allow for a natural pressure release, for 10 minutes, then quick release. Serve chilled.

Nutritional Info per Serving: Calories 127, Protein 3, Carbs 16, Fat 6

Chickpeas Stew

(Prep + Cook Time: 35 minutes / Servings: 2)

Ingredients:

½ lb. chickpeas, soaked
1 tomato, diced
1 oz. parsley, chopped
1 cup vegetable broth
½ onion, sliced

⅛ tsp cayenne pepper
1 tbsp butter
½ tbsp olive oil
Salt and black pepper, to taste

Directions:

1. Heat oil on SAUTÉ mode and add the onion. Stir-fry for 3-4 minutes.
2. Add the remaining ingredients, seal the lid and set the steam release handle.
3. Press the STEW button and set the cooking time to 30 minutes.
4. When ready, perform a quick release and serve hot.

Nutritional Info per Serving: Calories 363, Protein 22.3, Carbs 53.3, Fat 18.2

Beef Brisket Stew

(Prep + Cook Time: 95 minutes / Servings: 2)

Ingredients:

1 lb. beef brisket, sliced
1 tbsp. oil
½ tbsp. flour
1 garlic clove, minced
2 potatoes, cubed
½ onion, diced

1 carrot, peeled and chopped
1 celery stalk, chopped
½ tsp. Worcestershire sauce
1 cup beef stock
2 tbsp. tomato paste
½ tbsp. soy sauce

Directions:

1. Set your Instant Pot to SAUTÉ mode.
2. Heat the oil, and sauté the onions for 3 minutes. Stir in garlic, and cook for another minute. Add the beef, and brown for 5 minutes per side.
3. Next, add the carrot and celery, and cook for 2 more minutes. Stir in the remaining ingredients and seal the lid. Select MANUAL and cook on HIGH pressure for 70 minutes.
4. When ready, release the pressure naturally for 10 minutes. Serve and enjoy!

Nutritional Info per Serving: Calories 556, Protein 56, Carbs 40, Fat 18

Rice and Risotto

Basic Instant Pot White Rice

(Prep + Cook Time: 15 minutes / Servings: 2)

Ingredients:

½ cup white basmati rice
1 cup water

Salt and black pepper, to taste

Directions:

1. Combine the water and rice in your Instant Pot.
2. Season with some salt and pepper. Seal the lid, select MANUAL, and cook on LOW pressure for 8 minutes. When ready, release the pressure quickly.
3. Fluff the rice with a fork. Serve and enjoy!

Nutritional Info per Serving: Calories 225, Protein 4, Carbs 48, Fat 0.5

Instant Fried Rice with Peas

(Prep + Cook Time: 15 minutes / Servings: 2)

Ingredients:

½ tbsp. butter
½ onion, diced
1 egg
⅛ cup soy sauce

1 cup chicken stock
¼ cup peas
½ cup basmati rice
1 garlic clove, minced

Directions:

1. Set the Instant Pot to SAUTÉ mode and melt the butter.
2. Stir in the onion, and cook for 2 minutes. Add the garlic, and cook 1 minute.
3. Scramble the egg, add to the pot, and cook for an additional minute.
4. Stir in soy sauce, broth, and rice. Seal the lid, select RICE, and cook for 10 minutes.
5. When done, release the pressure quickly, open the lid and stir in the peas.
6. Then select SAUTÉ mode, and cook for 1 minute. Serve immediately.

Nutritional Info per Serving: Calories 251, Protein 7, Carbs 44, Fat 4.5

Sweet Rice in Coconut Milk

(Prep + Cook Time: 30 minutes / Servings: 2)

Ingredients:

1 cup water
½ cup rice
1 tbsp. sugar

Salt to taste
¼ can coconut milk

Directions:

1. Combine the water and rice in the Instant Pot, and seal the lid.
2. Select MANUAL, and cook on HIGH for 3 minutes.
3. When ready, do a natural pressure release for 10 minutes.
4. Carefully open the lid and stir in the remaining ingredients.
5. Seal the lid, and let rest for 10 minutes.
6. Serve and enjoy!

Nutritional Info per Serving: Calories 243, Protein 3, Carbs 45, Fat 7

Sesame Risotto

(Prep + Cook Time: 35 minutes / Servings: 2)

Ingredients:

6 oz. lamb, half-inch thick pieces
½ cup rice
1 ½ cup beef broth

¼ cup green peas
2 tbsp. sesame seeds
¼ tsp. thyme, dried

Directions:

1. Place the meat in the Instant Pot and add the beef broth.
2. Press MEAT and cook for 15 minutes. When done, do a quick steam release.
3. Remove the meat from the Pot, keep the liquid. Add the rice and green peas.
4. Season with salt and thyme. Stir well and add the meat.
5. Press RICE button and cook for 15 minutes. When done, perform a quick release. Sprinkle with sesame seeds and serve immediately.

Nutritional Info per Serving: Calories 463, Protein 31.3, Carbs 46.7, Fat 18.6

Mushroom and Spinach Risotto

(Prep + Cook Time: 25 minutes / Servings: 2)

Ingredients:

¼ cup onion, chopped
1 ½ cup veggie broth
2 oz. mushrooms, chopped
1 garlic clove, minced
⅛ cup lemon juice
½ tsp. thyme

1 cup spinach
¼ cup white wine
½ tbsp. oil
½ tbsp. butter
½ cup arborio rice
1 tbsp. nutritional yeast

Directions:

1. Set your Instant Pot to SAUTÉ mode.
2. Heat the oil, add the onion and garlic, and stir-fry for 3 minutes.
3. Add the mushrooms, thyme, rice, wine, and broth, and seal the lid.
4. Cook on HIGH on MANUAL for 5 minutes.
5. When done, release the pressure quickly for 10 minutes.
6. Carefully open the lid, and stir in spinach, butter, and yeast.
7. Serve and enjoy!

Nutritional Info per Serving: Calories 320, Protein 10, Carbs 45, Fat 8

French Onion Brown Rice

(Prep + Cook Time: 35 minutes / Servings: 2)

Ingredients:

1 cup veggie stock
1 cup French onion soup, condensed

1 cup brown rice
¼ cup butter

Directions:

1. Combine all ingredients in your Instant Pot. Seal the lid and select MANUAL.
2. Cook on HIGH pressure for 22 minutes. When ready, release the pressure naturally for 10 minutes, and enjoy.

Nutritional Info per Serving: Calories 513, Protein 9.5, Carbs 75, Fat 26

Mexican Chili Rice Casserole

(Prep + Cook Time: 35 minutes / Servings: 2)

Ingredients:

½ cup black beans, soaked
2 ½ cups water
1 tsp. chili powder
1 tsp. onion powder

3 oz. tomato paste
1 cup brown rice
½ tsp. minced garlic

Directions:

1. Place all ingredients in your Instant Pot.

2. Stir to combine. Seal the lid, select MANUAL and cook on HIGH pressure for 28 minutes.

3. When done, release the pressure quickly for 10 minutes.

4. Serve and enjoy!

Nutritional Info per Serving: Calories 322, Protein 6, Carbs 63, Fat 2

Edamame Arborio Risotto

(Prep + Cook Time: 30 minutes / Servings: 2)

Ingredients:

½ tbsp. butter
½ tbsp. oil
¼ cup white wine
½ cup edamame, thawed

1 tbsp. butter
1 cup chicken stock
½ onion, chopped
½ cup arborio rice

Directions:

1. Set your Instant Pot to SAUTÉ mode.

2. Heat the oil, and stir in the onion. Stir-fry for 3 minutes, until translucent.

3. Add the rice, and cook for 2 minutes.

4. Pour the wine, and cook until the rice absorbs it.

5. Next, pour the broth in, and seal the lid.

6. Select MANUAL mode, and cook on HIGH pressure for 8 minutes.

7. When ready, do a quick pressure release and stir in butter and edamame.

8. Serve and enjoy!

Nutritional Info per Serving: Calories 356, Protein 7, Carbs 54, Fat 10

Veggie Risotto

(Prep + Cook Time: 30 minutes / Servings: 2)

Ingredients:

½ cup arborio rice
1 cup chicken stock
⅛ cup heavy cream
½ carrot, peeled and shredded
½ onion, chopped
1 garlic clove, chopped

½ bell pepper, diced
2 oz. mushrooms, sliced
1 tbsp. butter
½ tbsp. olive oil
2 tbsp. Parmesan cheese

Directions:

1. Set your Instant Pot to SAUTÉ mode.
2. Heat the olive oil, and cook the onion and bell pepper for 3 minutes.
3. Stir in the garlic, and cook for 1 minute more.
4. Add the mushrooms and carrot, and cook for 3 minutes.
5. Stir in broth, heavy cream, and rice.
6. Seal the lid, select MANUAL, and cook for 12 minutes on HIGH.
7. When done, release the pressure quickly and carefully open the lid.
8. Stir in Parmesan and butter, and enjoy.

Nutritional Info per Serving: Calories 305, Protein 5, Carbs 48, Fat 4

Seafood Risotto

(Prep + Cook Time: 25 minutes / Servings: 4)

Ingredients:

½ cup rice
2 anchovies
2 oz. mussels
2 tbsp. olive oil
½ onion, chopped

1 garlic clove, crushed
½ oz. capers
½ tbsp. dried rosemary, chopped
½ tsp. ground chili pepper
Salt to taste

Directions:

1. Place the rice in your Instant Pot and add 1 cup of water.
2. Seal the lid and press MANUAL. Set to 6 minutes on HIGH pressure.
3. When done, perform a quick release and remove the rice.

4. Grease the bottom of the Instant Pot with oil and set on SAUTÉ mode

5. Add the garlic and onion and stir-fry them, stirring constantly for 3 minutes.

6. Add the mussels and rosemary and continue to cook for 8 more minutes.

7. Then, stir in the rice and season with salt and chili pepper.

8. Serve with anchovies and capers.

Nutritional Info per Serving: Calories 325, Protein 12.7, Carbs 38.3 Fat 11.1

Shrimp Risotto

(Prep + Cook Time: 20 minutes / Servings: 2)

Ingredients:

½ cup arborio rice
½ lb. shrimp, peeled and deveined
1 tbsp. white wine
½ onion, chopped
2 tbsp. butter, divided

⅛ cup fresh herbs
¼ cup Parmesan cheese
1 garlic clove, minced
1 cup chicken broth

Directions

1. Set your Instant Pot to SAUTÉ mode.

2. Melt half of the butter, and add the onions. Stir-fry for 3 minutes.

3. Add the garlic, and cook 1 minute more.

4. Pour the wine and add the rice, and cook for 3 minutes.

5. Stir in the remaining ingredients, except the remaining butter and cheese.

6. Seal the lid, select MANUAL, and cook on HIGH pressure for 5 minutes.

7. When done, release the pressure naturally for 10 minutes.

8. Carefully open the lid and stir in Parmesan and butter.

9. Serve and enjoy!

Nutritional Info per Serving: Calories 455, Protein 24, Carbs 55, Fat 15.4

Pasta

Mac and Cheese

(Prep + Cook Time: 15 minutes / Servings: 2)

Ingredients:

½ lb. macaroni
1 oz. fresh goat cheese, crumbled
½ tsp Dijon mustard
2 cups of water
¼ cup skim milk

½ tsp oregano, dried
½ tbsp vegetable oil
½ tsp sea salt
½ tsp Italian seasoning mix
1 tbsp extra virgin olive oil

Directions:

1. Pour 2 cups of water, and add the macaroni and vegetable oil.
2. Set to MANUAL, seal the lid and cook for 3 minutes.
3. When done, perform a quick release. Carefully open the lid.
4. Drain the macaroni in a large colander and set aside.
5. Press SAUTÉ, and add the olive oil, dijon mustard, milk, oregano, Italian seasoning mix, and salt.
6. Cook for 6 minutes, stirring constantly. Add the macaroni and stir.
7. Cook for 3 more minutes, then remove from the pot and top with fresh goat's cheese before serving.

Nutritional Info per Serving: Calories 487, Protein 15.1, Carbs 69.3, Fat 18.3

Beans Beef Pasta in Beer Sauce

(Prep + Cook Time: 20 minutes / Servings: 2)

Ingredients:

½ lb. ground beef
1 cup corn kernels
4 oz. pasta
½ bell pepper, chopped
1 tbsp. sweet paprika
7 oz. can kidney beans, drained

6 oz. ale
½ onion, chopped
½ tbsp. olive oil
1 tbsp. minced garlic
½ tsp. cumin
14 oz. can diced tomatoes

Directions:

1. Set your Instant Pot to SAUTÉ mode and heat the oil.
2. Place the beef and brown it for 3-5 minutes.
3. Add the onion and garlic, and cook for 3 more minutes.
4. Then, stir in the remaining ingredient. Seal the lid and select MANUAL mode.
5. Cook on HIGH pressure for 8 minutes.
6. When done, release the pressure quickly for 10 minutes and serve hot.

Nutritional Info per Serving: Calories 588, Protein 43, Carbs 88, Fat 21

Pasta with Fish Fillets

(Prep + Cook Time: 40 minutes / Servings: 2)

Ingredients:

½ lb. squid ink pasta
3 oz. trout fillet
½ cup olive oil
juice from ½ lemon

½ tsp. fresh rosemary, chopped
1 garlic clove, crushed and halved
1 tbsp. fresh parsley, chopped
Salt to taste

Directions:

1. In a large bowl, combine olive oil, lemon juice, 1 garlic clove, and rosemary.
2. Season with salt. Stir well.
3. Add in the fillets in this mixture and refrigerate for half hour.
4. Remove the fillets from the fridge and add to Instant Pot along with ½ cup of water.
5. Seal the lid, set the steam release handle and cook on MANUAL for 5 minutes.
6. When ready, perform a quick pressure release and add the squid ink pasta, and another cup of water.
7. Seal the lid, set the steam release handle and cook on MANUAL for 5 minutes.
8. Allow for a natural release.
9. Sprinkle with parsley and serve.

Nutritional Info per Serving: Calories 414, Protein 23.1, Carbs 49.1, Fat 17.3

Cannelloni with Spinach and Mushrooms

(Prep + Cook Time: 35 minutes / Servings: 2)

Ingredients:

½ pack of 8.8 oz cannelloni
6 oz. spinach, torn
3 oz. button mushrooms, sliced
1 ½ oz. ricotta cheese

1 oz. butter
½ cup of sour cream
¼ cup milk
baking sheet

Directions:

1. Press SAUTÉ, melt the butter and add the mushrooms.
2. Stir and cook until soft. Add the spinach and milk.
3. Cook for 5 minutes, stirring constantly.
4. Add the cheese and stir. Then press CANCEL.
5. Preheat oven to 400 degrees F and line parchment paper over a baking sheet.
6. Fill the cannelloni with the spinach mixture and place them on the baking sheet.
7. Bake for 18 minutes.
8. When ready, remove from the oven and top with sour cream.

Nutritional Info per Serving: Calories 436, Protein 13, Carbs 41.6, Fat 25.3

Alfredo and Chicken Fettuccine

(Prep + Cook Time: 10 minutes / Servings: 2)

Ingredients:

½ cup shredded chicken, cooked
4 oz. fettuccine

1 cup water
7 oz. Alfredo sauce

Directions:

1. Add the pasta, chicken, and water to your Instant Pot.
2. Seal the lid, select MANUAL, and cook on HIGH for 3 minutes.
3. When ready, release the pressure quickly. Stir in the sauce.
4. Serve immediately and top with freshly grated parmesan (optional).

Nutritional Info per Serving: Calories 490, Protein 27, Carbs 59, Fat 16

Tagliatelle with Mushrooms

(Prep + Cook Time: 20 minutes / Servings: 4)

Ingredients:

½ lb. tagliatelle
3 oz frozen mixed mushrooms
¼ cup feta cheese
¼ cup grated parmesan cheese

¼ cup cooking cream
1 tbsp butter, unsalted
1 garlic clove, crushed
½ tbsp Italian seasoning mix

Directions:

1. Press SAUTÉ, melt the butter and add the garlic. Fry for 2 minutes, stirring continuously. Add the feta, parmesan, and cooking cream. Give it a good stir and cook for 3 more minutes. Add the mushrooms and cook for 6 minutes.

2. Press Cancel. Add the tagliatelle and 1 cup of water. Set on MANUAL, seal the lid and set the timer to 5 minutes. When ready, allow for a natural pressure release, for 10 minutes and serve.

Nutritional Info per Serving: Calories 418, Protein 21.3, Carbs 53.1, Fat 17.1

Beef and Tomato Sauce Macaroni

(Prep + Cook Time: 35 minutes / Servings: 2)

Ingredients:

½ pack macaroni, 16 oz.
3 oz. beef, braising steak cut into chunks
½ onion, chopped
½ tomato, diced
½ tbsp. tomato paste

1 tbsp. butter
½ tsp. cayenne pepper
1 bay leaf
½ tbsp. vegetable oil

Directions:

1. Grease the bottom of the Instant Pot with oil. Select SAUTÉ and add the onion. Fry until translucent, stirring constantly. Add the butter, tomato, tomato paste, salt, black and cayenne pepper. Cook until the tomato softens, stirring occasionally. Add the beef chunks and ½ cup of water. Stir and seal the lid. Cook for 15 minutes on MEAT mode.

2. When done, perform a quick release and remove the meat; set it aside.

3. Place the macaroni in the steel insert and add 2 cups of water. Press MANUAL and cook for 5 minutes. When ready, perform a quick release. Transfer the macaroni to a large bowl and pour in the beef sauce.

Nutritional Info per Serving: Calories 523, Protein 26.1, Carbs 78.1, Fat 14.3

Garlic Beef and Onion Spaghetti

(Prep + Cook Time: 20 minutes / Servings: 2)

Ingredients:

½ lb. beef, chopped into small pieces
4 oz. spaghetti, uncooked
½ onion, chopped
1 garlic clove, minced

1 tbsp. oil
1 cup broth
Salt and black pepper, to taste

Directions:

1. Set your Instant Pot to SAUTÉ mode and pour the olive oil in. Heat the olive oil. Add the onion, and cook for 3 minutes, until translucent. Add the garlic, and cook for 1 minute more.

2. Place the beef, and cook until browned, for about 3-5 minutes per side.

3. Pour the broth and add the pasta. Season with salt and pepper.

4. Seal the lid, press MANUAL and cook on HIGH for 10 minutes. When done, release the pressure quickly and serve immediately.

Nutritional Info per Serving: Calories 512, Protein 51.5, Carbs 23, Fat 36.3

Seafood Pasta

(Prep + Cook Time: 25 minutes / Servings: 2)

Ingredients:

½ lb. squid ink pasta, cooked
½ lb. fresh seafood mix
⅛ cup olive oil
1 garlic clove, crushed

½ tbsp. fresh parsley, chopped
½ tbsp. fresh rosemary, chopped
¼ cup white wine
Salt to taste

Directions:

1. Grease the bottom of the Instant Pot with 1 tbsp. olive oil.

2. Press SAUTÉ and add the garlic. Stir-fry for 2 minutes.

3. Add seafood mix, parsley, rosemary, olive oil, wine, half a cup of water and salt. Stir well.

4. Seal the lid and set the steam release handle. Press MANUAL and set to 5 minutes.

5. Once done, perform a quick release and open the lid to add the cooked pasta. Stir and serve immediately.

Nutritional Info per Serving: Calories 265, Protein 25.8, Carbs 23.9, Fat 12.5

Onion and Beef Cheesy Pasta

(Prep + Cook Time: 30 minutes / Servings: 2)

Ingredients:

¼ lb. ground beef
1 beef bouillon cubes
2 oz. cheddar cheese, grated

½ packet onion soup mix
¼ pound elbow macaroni
1 ½ cups water

Directions:

1. Set your Instant Pot to SAUTÉ mode. Place the beef and cook it until brown.

2. Stir in bouillon, onion soup mix, water, and macaroni.

3. Seal the lid, and select MANUAL. Cook on HIGH pressure for 5 minutes.

4. When ready, release the pressure naturally for 10 minutes. Open the lid and stir in the cheddar cheese before serving.

Nutritional Info per Serving: Calories 462, Protein 35, Carbs 43, Fat 15

Spicy Mexican Beef Pasta

(Prep + Cook Time: 10 minutes / Servings: 2)

Ingredients:

¼ lb. ground beef
1 cup water
4 oz. can black beans
½ cup Doritos

4 oz. salsa
½ packet taco seasoning
4 oz. pasta
¼ cup shredded cheddar

Directions:

1. Set the Instant Pot to SAUTÉ mode and coat it with cooking spray.

2. Add the beef and taco seasoning, and cook until browned.

3. Next, add the pasta, beans, salsa, and water to the pot. Seal the lid.

4. Select MANUAL. Cook on HIGH for 4 minutes. Once done, release the pressure naturally for 10 minutes. Arrange Doritos in a baking dish, top with the pasta, and sprinkle with cheese. Then, pour water into your Instant Pot, and place the dish inside.

5. Seal the lid, set on MANUAL and cook on HIGH pressure for 5 minutes.

6. When ready, do a quick release and serve immediately!

Nutritional Info per Serving: Calories 425, Protein 25, Carbs 55, Fat 21

Creamy Bowtie Pasta with Shrimp

(Prep + Cook Time: 15 minutes / Servings: 2)

Ingredients:

4 oz. bowtie pasta
½ yellow onion, chopped
6 oz. frozen shrimp
½ tbsp. olive oil

¼ cup heavy cream
½ cup grated Parmesan cheese
1 ½ cups chicken broth
1 garlic clove, minced
Salt and black pepper, to taste

Directions:

1. Set the Instant Pot to SAUTÉ mode and heat the oil.
2. Stir in the onion and cook for 3 minutes.
3. Add the garlic, and cook for 1 minute more.
4. Stir in shrimp, pasta, broth, salt, and pepper.
5. Cook for 7 minutes on MANUAL mode on high pressure.
6. When ready, release the pressure quickly for 10 minutes.
7. Drain the pasta and shrimp, and return them to the pot.
8. Stir in Parmesan and cream, and cook on SAUTÉ mode for 2 minutes.
9. Serve immediately and enjoy.

Nutritional Info per Serving: Calories 511 Protein 33, Carbs 47, Fat 22

Chicken Cordon Bleu Pasta

(Prep + Cook Time: 50 minutes / Servings: 2)

Ingredients:

¼ cup breadcrumbs
¼ lb. chicken breast, cut into strips
¼ lb. ham, cubed
4 oz. Swiss cheese
½ cup chicken broth

½ tbsp. butter
2 oz. gouda cheese
4 oz. pasta
2 oz. heavy cream

Directions:

1. Combine pasta, broth, chicken, and ham in your Instant Pot.
2. Seal the lid, press MANUAL and cook on HIGH for 25 minutes.

3. When done, release the pressure quickly.
4. Stir in the remaining ingredients, except the breadcrumbs.
5. Cook on SAUTÉ for 3 minutes.
6. Sprinkle the breadcrumbs on top and serve.

Nutritional Info per Serving: Calories 574, Protein 47, Carbs 43, Fat 31

Roasted Veggies Pasta

(Prep + Cook Time: 25 minutes / Servings: 2)

Ingredients:

2 cups pasta
½ tomato, chopped
1 garlic clove, minced
½ onion, chopped
½ bell pepper, chopped
½ zucchini, chopped

¼ cup grated Parmesan cheese
1 ½ cups chicken broth
¼ cup heavy cream
Salt and black pepper
½ tbsp. oil

Directions:

1. Set your Instant Pot to SAUTÉ mode.
2. Heat the oil, and cook the onion and bell pepper for 3 minutes.
3. Add the garlic, and cook for 1 minute more.
4. Add the zucchini and cook for 1 minute.
5. Stir in pasta, broth, and heavy cream, and season with salt and pepper.
6. Seal the lid, select MANUAL, and cook on HIGH for 5 minutes.
7. When done, release the pressure naturally for 10 minutes.
8. Open the lid, stir in the Parmesan cheese and serve immediately.

Nutritional Info per Serving: Calories 420, Protein 5, Carbs 57, Fat 8

Fish and Seafood

Shrimp Creole

(Prep + Cook Time: 20 minutes / Servings: 2)

Ingredients:

½ lb. jumbo shrimp, peeled, deveined
1 celery stalk, diced
1 garlic clove, minced
1 tsp. olive oil

½ tsp. thyme
½ onion, diced
14 oz. can tomatoes, diced
½ bell pepper, diced

Directions:

1. Set the Instant Pot to SAUTÉ mode and heat the oil.
2. Stir in the onion, garlic, and celery, and cook for 3 minutes.
3. Add the remaining ingredients. Give it a good stir to combine.
4. Seal the lid and select MANUAL. Cook on HIGH for 1 minute.
5. When done, release the pressure quickly. Set it to SAUTÉ mode again, and cook until the liquid is reduced, at least 10 minutes.

Nutritional Info per Serving: Calories 264, Protein 31, Carbs 24, Fat 4.5

Halibut Dijon

(Prep + Cook Time: 5 minutes / Servings: 2)

Ingredients:

½ tbsp. Dijon mustard

2 halibut fillets

Directions:

1. Pour 1 cup of water into your Instant Pot.
2. Brush the fish fillets with mustard.
3. Arrange the fish in the steaming basket.
4. Seal the lid, and select MANUAL. Cook on HIGH for 3 minutes.
5. When ready, release the pressure quickly and serve immediately.

Nutritional Info per Serving: Calories 191, Protein 41, Carbs 0.1, Fat 2

Quick Salmon and Broccoli

(Prep + Cook Time: 5 minutes / Servings: 2)

Ingredients:

5 oz. broccoli florets
2 salmon fillets
1 cup water

½ tsp. garlic powder
Salt and pepper, to taste

Directions:

1. Season the salmon with garlic powder, salt, and pepper.
2. Sprinkle the broccoli with salt and pepper, as well.
3. Pour the water into your Instant Pot.
4. Arrange the salmon in the steaming basket and scatter the broccoli around the fillets.
5. Seal the lid, and select MANUAL. Cook on HIGH for 2 minutes.
6. When ready, release the pressure quickly and serve immediately.

Nutritional Info per Serving: Calories 119, Protein 16, Carbs 5, Fat 5

Cajun Shrimp and Asparagus

(Prep + Cook Time: 25 minutes / Servings: 2)

Ingredients:

½ tbsp. Cajun seasoning
½ lb. shrimp, peeled and deveined
½ tsp. olive oil

½ asparagus bunch, 12, trimmed
1 ½ cups water

Directions:

1. Pour the water into your Instant Pot.
2. Arrange the asparagus on the rack, in a single layer.
3. Place the shrimp on top.
4. Drizzle with olive oil, and season with Cajun seasoning.
5. Seal the lid, and select the STEAM mode. Cook on LOW for 2 minutes.
6. When ready, release the pressure quickly.

Nutritional Info per Serving: Calories 329, Protein 56, Carbs 11, Fat 6

Mackerel with Spinach and Potatoes

(Prep + Cook Time: 30 minutes / Servings: 2)

Ingredients:

2 medium-sized mackerels, skin on
½ lb. fresh spinach, torn
2 potatoes, peeled and sliced
¼ cup olive oil

1 garlic clove, crushed
½ tbsp. rosemary, dried, chopped
1 spring fresh mint leaves, chopped
Juice of ½ lemon

Directions:

1. Grease the bottom of the Instant Pot with 2 tbsp. of olive oil.
2. Press the SAUTÉ button and add garlic and rosemary.
3. Stir-fry for a minute and add the spinach.
4. Sprinkle with salt and cook for 5 more minutes, stirring occasionally.
5. Remove the spinach from the cooker and set aside.
6. Add the remaining olive oil to the pot and make a layer in the potatoes.
7. Place the fish and drizzle with lemon juice and sea salt.
8. Pour in ½ cup of water and seal the lid. Adjust the steam release handle and press STEAM, setting the cooking time for 8 minutes.
9. When ready, release the steam naturally and transfer the fish and the potatoes to a serving plate. Serve with the spinach.

Nutritional Info per Serving: Calories 267, Protein 14.5, Carbs 23.5, Fat 12.1

Green Salmon

(Prep + Cook Time: 25 minutes / Servings: 2)

Ingredients:

½ lb. salmon fillets, boneless
½ lb. fresh spinach, torn
1 ½ tbsp. olive oil
½ garlic cloves, finely chopped

½ tbsp. lemon juice
½ tbsp. fresh rosemary, chopped
Sea salt and black pepper to taste

Directions:

1. Grease the bottom of the Instant Pot with 1 tbsp. olive oil.
2. Place the salmon fillets and season with rosemary, salt and pepper.
3. Drizzle with lemon juice, add a half cup of water and close.

4. Set the steam release handle and press the MANUAL button.
5. Cook on HIGH pressure for 4 minutes.
6. When done, press CANCEL and turn off the Instant Pot.
7. In a large pot, place the torn spinach and cover with water.
8. Bring to a boil and cook for 2 -3 minutes or until tender. Drain in a colander.
9. Remove the salmon from the Instant Pot and place the spinach at the bottom.
10. Pour half a cup of water and add garlic.
11. Top with salmon and set to SAUTÉ mode. Cook for 7 - 8 minutes more.

Nutritional Info per Serving: Calories 451, Protein 41.1, Carbs 15.3, Fat 25.8

Instant Shrimp Casserole with Tomatoes

(Prep + Cook Time: 35 minutes / Servings: 2)

Ingredients:

1 lb. tomatoes, chopped

1 lb. shrimp, peeled and deveined

⅛ cup chopped cilantro

½ tbsp. lime juice

½ onion, chopped

1 tbsp. olive oil

½ jalapeño, diced

½ cup shredded cheddar cheese

¼ cup clam juice

1 garlic clove, minced

Directions:

1. Set your Instant Pot to SAUTÉ mode.
2. Heat the olive oil, and sauté the onion for 3 minutes.
3. Add the garlic, and cook for 1 minute more.
4. Stir in tomatoes, clam juice, and cilantro.
5. Seal the lid, select MANUAL mode and cook on HIGH for 9 minutes.
6. Once done, release the pressure naturally for 10 minutes.
7. Stir in cilantro and shrimp, and cook on HIGH pressure for 1 minute.
8. Next, stir in cheddar and sprinkle with lemon juice.
9. Once the tomatoes have softened and the liquid has evaporated, add the remaining ingredients. Press CANCEL, seal the lid and set the steam handle.
10. Set on STEW mode and cook for 16 minutes. Serve hot.

Nutritional Info per Serving: Calories 310, Protein 22, Carbs 17, Fat 16

Caramelized Tilapia Fillets

(Prep + Cook Time: 55 minutes / Servings: 2)

Ingredients:

½ lb. tilapia fillets
½ scallion, minced
½ cup coconut water
1 garlic clove, minced
¼ cup water

1 ½ tbsp. fish sauce
⅛ cup sugar
Salt and black pepper, to taste
½ red chili, minced

Directions:

1. Marinate the tilapia in fish sauce, salt, pepper, and garlic for 30 minutes on the counter. Combine the water and sugar in your Instant Pot.

2. Set on SAUTÉ mode and cook until caramelized.

3. Add the fish and coconut water in the Instant Pot.

4. Seal the lid, and select MANUAL. Cook on HIGH for 10 minutes.

5. When ready, do a quick release and top with spring onions and red chili.

Nutritional Info per Serving: Calories 150, Protein 21, Carbs 18, Fat 2

Instant Crunchy Tuna

(Prep + Cook Time: 5 minutes / Servings: 2)

Ingredients:

1 can of 5 oz. tuna
½ cup grated cheddar cheese
1 cup crushed saltine crackers

1 tbsp. butter
1 garlic clove, minced

Directions:

1. Set on SAUTÉ mode.

2. Melt the butter, and cook the garlic for 1 minute.

3. Add tuna, cheddar, and crackers.

4. Sauté for 2 minutes.

5. Serve immediately and enjoy!

Nutritional Info per Serving: Calories 143, Protein 9, Carbs 13, Fat 3

Cheesy Haddock

(Prep + Cook Time: 35 minutes / Servings: 2)

Ingredients:

6 oz. haddock fillets
¼ cup heavy cream
½ tsp. ground ginger

2 oz. cheddar cheese, grated
Salt and black pepper, to taste
½ tbsp. butter

Directions:

1. Combine the ginger, salt, and pepper, in a small bowl.
2. Rub the haddock with the spice mixture.
3. Melt the butter in the Instant Pot on SAUTÉ mode.
4. Add the haddock, and cook on SAUTÉ for 2 minutes per side.
5. Pour the cream and cheese over the fillets.
6. Seal the lid, select MANUAL, and cook on STEW for 10 minutes.
7. When done, release the pressure naturally for 10 minutes.

Nutritional Info per Serving: Calories 194, Protein 18, Carbs 6.5, Fat 18

Catfish with Dill and Soy

(Prep + Cook Time: 15 minutes / Servings: 2)

Ingredients:

½ tbsp. olive oil
1 tbsp. soy sauce
⅛ cup water

1 tsp. chopped dill
2 catfish fillets
1 garlic clove, minced

Directions:

1. Heat the oil in your Instant Pot on SAUTÉ mode.
2. Add the garlic, and cook for 1 minute.
3. Pour the soy sauce and add the dill.
4. Add the catfish and season with salt and pepper.
5. Cook for about 4 minutes per side. Serve with green salad or potatoes.

Nutritional Info per Serving: Calories 103, Protein 11, Carbs 2.5, Fat 5

Buttery Crab Legs

(Prep + Cook Time: 10 minutes / Servings: 2)

Ingredients:

¼ cup butter

1 garlic clove, minced

1 ½ lb. crab legs

½ tsp. olive oil

Directions:

1. Pour 2 cups of water into your Instant Pot. Place the crab legs in the steaming basket. Seal the lid, and select the STEAM mode.

2. Cook for 3 - 4 minutes. Transfer to a plate. Set the Instant Pot to SAUTÉ.

3. Pour the oil and add the butter. Heat until the butter is melted.

4. Add garlic, and cook for 1 minute. Pour garlic butter sauce over the crab legs.

Nutritional Info per Serving: Calories 293, Protein 35, Carbs 3, Fat 6

Desserts

Sweet Tapioca Pudding

(Prep + Cook Time: 10 minutes / Servings: 2)

Ingredients:

1 cup almond milk
¼ cup sugar
¼ cup tapioca pearls

¼ cup sugar
¼ cup water
¼ tsp. vanilla extract

Directions:

1. Pour the water into your Instant Pot.
2. In a heatproof bowl, combine all of the remaining ingredients.
3. Place the bowl inside your Instant Pot.
4. Seal the lid, select MANUAL, and cook on HIGH for 8 minutes.
5. When ready, release the pressure naturally for 10 minutes. Serve and enjoy!

Nutritional Info per Serving: Calories 187, Protein 2.5, Carbs 39, Fat 2.5

Dark Chocolate Fondue

(Prep + Cook Time: 5 minutes / Servings: 2)

Ingredients:

1 cup water
½ tsp. sugar

2 oz. coconut cream
4 oz. dark chocolate, chopped

Directions:

1. Pour the water into your Instant Pot.
2. In a heatproof bowl, add the chocolate, sugar, and coconut cream.
3. Place in the Instant Pot.
4. Seal the lid, select MANUAL, and cook for 2 minutes.
5. When ready, do a quick release and carefully open the lid.
6. Give it a good stir and serve immediately.

Nutritional Info per Serving: Calories 216, Protein 2, Carbs 11, Fat 17

Simple Mango-Flavored Cake

(Prep + Cook Time: 50 minutes / Servings: 2)

Ingredients:

1 cup flour
⅛ cup coconut oil
½ tsp. mango syrup
½ tsp. baking powder
Salt to taste

⅛ tsp. baking soda
½ cup milk
1 cup water
¼ cup sugar

Directions:

1. Grease a baking pan with cooking spray.

2. Pour the water in your Instant Pot.

3. Whisk together all of the remaining ingredients, in a bowl.

4. Transfer the batter to the prepared baking pan.

5. Place on the trivet and then inside the pot. Seal the lid and select MANUAL.

6. Cook on HIGH pressure for 35 minutes. When done, release the pressure quickly.

7. Remove the pie from the pot, transfer to a serving platter and refrigerate overnight.

Nutritional Info per Serving: Calories 443, Protein 4, Carbs 78, Fat 14

Crème Brûlée

(Prep + Cook Time: 12 minutes / Servings: 2)

Ingredients:

4 egg yolks
2 ½ cups of heavy cream

½ vanilla bean, split lengthwise
¾ cup sugar, divided

Directions:

1. In a large bowl, combine the egg yolks, heavy cream and ½ cup of sugar. Beat with electric mixer.

2. Scrape the seeds out of the vanilla bean and add them to the heavy cream mixture. Add salt and beat again.

3. Pour the mixture into four standard-sized ramekins; set aside.

4. Take 4x12 inches long pieces of aluminum foil, and roll them up in snake-shaped pieces.

5. Curl into circles, pinching the ends together. Place at the bottom of the Instant Pot.

6. Place each ramekin on aluminum circle, and pour water to cover ⅓ of the way. Then pour the egg mixture.

7. Press MANUAL and cook on HIGH pressure for 7 minutes.

8. Allow for a natural pressure release for 10 minutes, and then perform a quick release.

9. Remove the ramekins from the Pot, and add 1 tbsp. of sugar in each ramekin.

10. Burn the surface with a culinary torch until lightly brown.

11. Serve cool.

Nutritional Info per Serving: Calories 231, Protein 14.5, Carbs 19.1, Fat 10.3

Wild Berries Pancakes

(Prep + Cook Time: 20 minutes / Servings: 2)

Ingredients:

½ cup buckwheat flour
1 tbsp. baking powder
1 cup skim milk
1 egg

½ tsp. salt
½ tbsp. vanilla sugar
½ cup yogurt
½ cup fresh wild berries

Directions:

1. In a medium-sized bowl, mix the milk and the egg, and beat with an electric mixer until foamy.

2. Gradually add flour and continue to beat.

3. Add baking powder, vanilla sugar and salt.

4. Keep beating 3 more minutes until batter is formed.

5. Grease the stainless steel insert with oil.

6. Spoon 2 tbsp. of batter into the pot for every pancake.

7. Seal the lid, and press MANUAL. Cook on LOW pressure for 5 minutes.

8. When ready, perform a quick release.

9. Repeat the process with the remaining batter.

10. Top each pancake with 1 tbsp. of yogurt and wild berries.

11. Transfer the strudels to a serving plate with the help of a spatula.

Nutritional Info per Serving: Calories 151, Protein 8.8 g, Carbs 21.1 g, Fat 2.6 g

Ricotta Cake with Apples

(Prep + Cook Time: 5 minutes / Servings: 2)

Ingredients:

⅛ cup sugar
2 apples, one diced and one sliced
1 egg
½ cup flour
½ cup ricotta

1 ½ tbsp. oil
1 tsp. baking powder
½ tbsp. lemon juice
½ tsp. baking soda
½ tsp. vanilla

Directions:

1. Pour 2 cups of water into your Instant Pot.
2. Line a baking dish with parchment paper.
3. Arrange the sliced apples at the bottom. Sprinkle with lemon juice.
4. Whisk the remaining ingredients in a bowl, including the diced apple.
5. Pour the batter over the apples.
6. Place the pan inside the Instant Pot.
7. Seal the lid, select MANUAL, and cook on HIGH for 20 minutes.
8. When ready, do a quick pressure release.
9. Serve and enjoy!

Nutritional Info per Serving: Calories 463, Protein 13, Carbs 56, Fat 19

Chocolate Molten Lava Cake

(Prep + Cook Time: 25 minutes / Servings: 2)

Ingredients:

¼ cup powdered sugar
1 tsp. vanilla extract
4 tbsp. butter

2 tbsp. flour
1 egg
½ cup chocolate chips, melted

Directions:

1. Pour 1 cup of water into your Instant Pot. Grease 2 ramekins.
2. Whisk all of the ingredients together in a bowl.
3. Transfer to the ramekins. Arrange the ramekins on the trivet.

4. Seal the lid, select MANUAL, and cook on HIGH for 7 minutes.

5. When ready, release the pressure naturally.

6. Carefully open the lid and serve immediately.

Nutritional Info per Serving: Calories 528, Protein 6.6, Carbs 48 Fat 29.3

Instant Brownies

(Prep + Cook Time: 45 minutes / Servings: 2)

Ingredients:

½ tbsp. honey
¼ cup melted butter
½ cup sugar
⅛ tsp. salt

⅛ cup cocoa powder
½ cup flour
1 egg
½ tsp. baking powder

Directions:

1. Pour 1 cup of water into your Instant Pot.

2. Mix the ingredients in a bowl, until well combined.

3. Grease a pan with cooking spray.

4. Pour the batter in it.

5. Place it in your Instant Pot, and seal the lid.

6. Select MANUAL, and cook on HIGH for 35 minutes.

7. When ready, do a quick pressure release.

8. Serve immediately.

Nutritional Info per Serving: Calories 530, Protein 8, Carbs 75, Fat 25

Conclusion

I hope you've enjoyed my Instant Pot recipes for two. And that you've worked your way through all of the amazing recipes in my book! My recipes and meal ideas are here to inspire you and show you exactly how comfortable and pleasant it is to cook using the Instant Pot. Along the way, you'll no doubt have come up with some own tricks and tips for using your Instant Pot to its full advantage.

Cooking for two is just as much fun as preparing for a crowd…with all the same delicious flavors and tasty dishes. Don't let a recipe that's been created for more than two put you off. You can either adjust the number of ingredients you use. Or you can anticipate getting more than one meal from a recipe!

Made in the USA
Middletown, DE
24 January 2019